2116 8x —

OCT 2003

TROPHY MAN

the surprising secrets of
black women who marry well

BELLWOOD PUBLIC LIBRARY

Joy McElroy

A FIRESIDE BOOK
Published by Simon & Schuster
NEW YORK · LONDON · TORONTO · SYDNEY · SINGAPORE

FIRESIDE
Rockefeller Center
1230 Avenue of the Americas
New York, NY 10020

Copyright © 2002 by Dr. Joy McElroy
All rights reserved,
including the right of reproduction
in whole or in part in any form.

FIRESIDE and colophon are registered trademarks
of Simon & Schuster, Inc.

For information about special discounts for bulk purchases,
please contact Simon & Schuster Special Sales:
1-800-456-6798 or business@simonandschuster.com

Designed by Adam W. Cohen

Manufactured in the United States of America

10 9 8 7 6 5 4 3 2 1

Library of Congress Cataloging-in-Publication Data
McElroy, Joy A.
    Trophy man : the surprising secrets of black women who marry well / Joy A. McElroy.
        p. cm.
    "A Fireside book."
    1. Man-woman relationships—United States. 2. Mate selection—United States. 3. African
American women. 4. African American men. 5. Marriage—United States. I. Title.

HQ801 .M48755 2002
646.7'7—dc21   2002019712

ISBN 0-7432-1305-X

This book is dedicated to:

Harvey S. McElroy, the original trophy man, and my mother, Louise Penny McElroy, two loving parents who gave my sister and me a happy and stable childhood and a firm foundation for a closely knit and strong adulthood.

My husband, Loi M. Chang-Stroman, a modern (yet traditional) version of a trophy man.

"My boys," Loi Harvey and August Gabriel (two little trophy men in training).

646.77
MRE
2002

Acknowledgments

Many interviews, multiple stories, and much advice came from countless women as I researched this book. It was truly a group effort, and above all, I thank the women whose patience, support, and cooperation helped launch me on the path of delivering the message. I thank you, I love you, and I hope I didn't irritate you too much.

Many heartfelt thanks to my husband, "my pinch-hit editor," for helping me through the long months of writing, revising and hashing through, and for being an armchair critic. I appreciate your support, love, and encouragement.

Thank you to all of my girlfriends, especially those who read through the rough cut, taught me that the message is universal, and showed me that in true friendship, there are no age or distance limitations. They provided truthful, and consequently, often humorous advice.

Thanks to my closest girlfriends who did not laugh when I first told them I wanted to be a writer.

I especially want to express gratitude and thanks to my agent, Ms. Claudia Menza, who took me on, understood the concept, and gave me a chance. You are truly a fairy godmother. "They like me? They really like me!"

Many, many thanks to my editor at Simon & Schuster, Cherise Grant, "a little wonder woman." Her wise counsel and support made the idea of *Trophy Man* a reality. You are like a little sister with big-sister advice.

Much thanks to Soni Edwards, my typist with "fingers of fury."

Last but not least, many thanks to all of the trophy men out there, young and old. You know who you are. Although it's hard to "do the right thing," you take the high ground. Women will always love you for it.

Contents

CONTENTS

Contents

TROPHY MAN

INTRODUCTION

The more you know, the less you need.
—AUSTRALIAN ABORIGINAL SAYING

IT'S HAPPENED TO ALL OF US AT SOME TIME OR ANOTHER. IT might have been in a crowded restaurant, while waiting in line at the movies, or perhaps at a friend's wedding reception. You see a beautiful Black couple—golden, really. She seems self-confident, happy, and adored by her man. He in turn, isn't necessarily handsome, but definitely refined looking. You notice the Mercedes keychain and her simple wedding band. He holds her hand, focuses intently on what she's saying, and beams with pride as they chat and laugh with their friends.

You find yourself eavesdropping. He mentions the kids joining them later on his corporate retreat. She begins to banter about a recent election and how it might affect the local economy. He listens attentively and then agrees. Their conversation is meaningful and effortless.

Something about the two of them is intriguing. They're so in tune with each other and so comfortable with each other. You wonder, Who are these people? Where did they come from? But most of all, How did they connect?

◆ 1

And while you're looking closely without trying to be too obvious, it occurs to you that he's the kind of man you've always envisioned for yourself. Not this exact man, but rather the same kind of man—a "trophy man."

A trophy man is not just a guy with good looks and money, because you're well beyond that. Instead, he's a good man, one who treats you with kindness and respect. He includes you and considers you. He's your friend and companion. He's a man who is educated and still wants to learn new things. A man who's intelligent and ambitious. He has morals and wants to do right by his family. He has a career that he's proud of, can take care of his family, and understands finances. He knows exactly what money is and what it isn't. He's well groomed, appealing, and well dressed. He works at being healthy and he wants to be happy. He's socialized, polished, and outgoing.

We've all seen the woman with the trophy-man husband. And perhaps what always grabs our attention is the fact that she isn't so different from us. In fact, she seems quite ordinary. Invariably, we watch her from a distance, picking apart and analyzing each and every fine detail we're able to get from a glance. She's not necessarily a stunning beauty. She isn't a circuit-breaking conversationalist or a social butterfly. But something sets her apart from the norm. She's considered a member of the inner circle of married women—not just married, but also married well.

We wonder, What's she have that I don't? How did she nab her trophy man? Where did she meet him? What made him decide that she was the one? It's perfectly natural to wonder what special attributes made her attractive and desirable. We all learn what works by looking at success stories of other women who have made it. Even as children we learn to emulate what works. We're copycats by nature. Remember playing dress-up in your mom's clothes? Or visually mapping the cover girl's face the first time you tried applying makeup?

The idea for this book started innocently enough, when a younger friend asked me how I'd met my husband. I could tell her question wasn't just ordinary chitchat. She was personally interested and wanted some sisterly advice. What struck me wasn't so much the question, but that *she'd* asked it. She was pretty, educated, intelligent, well traveled, and had a great job. I admired her. She was the last woman I'd have expected to be curious about how to meet a man or find a husband. But then I thought of myself and my circle of friends. It was difficult to find a nice, normal guy who shared similar values and wanted the same things out of life.

So, I sat down and thought about whether there was a set of character traits or hand-me-down secrets that we who married well knew of and could share with women seeking a mate. I took a select group of women who've married well and asked them hundreds of specific questions. Not fluff, but the real deal that all women wonder about in the back of their minds: How they'd met their trophy husband, how they'd presented and carried themselves while dating, and what factors might have led to their marriage. How soon did she sleep with him? How could she stand his mother? Did he wine and dine her, or string her along? Did she string him along or play hard to get?

Over the past five years, I sat down with a lot of girlfriends, coworkers, club members, and mentors. At least a hundred women were interviewed, and more than half of those women answered a sixty-page questionnaire. I got on their nerves and inflamed many with the questions I asked. "What's wrong with you, asking that stuff?" they'd argue, only half joking. "I'm not telling my business." Sisters don't put their business in the street, especially not sisters with a lot on the ball. I remember a psychiatrist, short-Afroed and elegant, telling me she understood exactly where I was trying to go, but she wasn't going there with me. While some fussed, others treated me like I was Oprah and bent over backward to accommodate me.

A few women were recently married, still in the "magnificent, plump, sweet, and juicy" phase of being newly wed. Others had been "good-and-married" for years, long after the sheen had worn off and the serious and difficult business of love began. Some were beyond affluence, with husbands who, yes, had their own plane. The only thing their minds fretted over was how to decorate their summer home or when to reserve their time-share. Others were comfortably ordinary folks, with homes not far from where they'd grown up, driving a family minivan, and complaining about the power struggle at PTA meetings. All were real Black women who realized the value that comes from speaking truthfully about what makes a man good and a marriage better.

In this book, you'll learn where they first met their husbands, and what attributes set these women apart from other girlfriends their husbands left behind. You'll learn how family background, appearances, sex, religion, money, and education played in the process. Once you see what it takes, you can decide if you're one of the women who are willing to do what it takes to marry a trophy man.

Some brothers will take issue with this book. Many women will be equally rattled. Frankly, I expect a lot of sisters are going to be mad. They'll argue that books like this throw women back into the dark ages, and that the women's movement and the sexual revolution changed women's focus from marrying well, or catching the man of their dreams, to taking care of themselves. And of course, without question, a woman doesn't need a husband to be whole. In fact, the wise woman will find happiness within herself first. We all know women who are successful, trend-setting, and very much single.

But ladies, let's face the plain truth: For many of us, success includes a husband and an ideal marriage. And none of us should be ashamed of wanting a husband, and a good husband at that! In fact, a successful, happy marriage requires that both partners be equal with one another when it comes to ambitions and goals.

While I was interviewing an older woman, she made reference to a passage in the Bible about a woman being yoked with her husband. I naively thought, There is no way I can put something in this book about being "yoked." Women will think I'm out of my mind. This is a new day and age, after all. Much to my surprise, while reviewing some astute recommendations I'd received from my editor, I came across this phrase: "Couples should not be unequally yoked." At that point it became very clear what the older woman was talking about. A woman has every right to want the best for herself, especially if she demands the best from herself. If she is working like a dog at a demanding job and striving to put away some money and build a life, she not only wants a man who is willing and able to do the same, but she should demand it.

I hate to say it, but many men cannot handle a woman who is more successful or financially secure than they are. You can try to be loving and cooperative and nurturing as much as you want, but these are the men who will resent you because you are successful, and who are likely to feel intimidated by you. Nobody wants a deadbeat or a hanger-on, especially not a trophy woman who is looking for a trophy man. On the flip side of the coin, some sisters have transformed themselves into screeching, overbearing, self-centered, overworked, and neurotic bitches. Who wants an overprogrammed, smart-alecky, unhappy woman? Can you blame these men?

There will be some women reading these pages who would agree that a trophy man is what they would ideally aim for, but who don't believe that he exists. There was a cute commercial on television several months ago that showed how being too successful could backfire. An Internet company launched their premier website and, within the first few minutes, got thousands of orders that they could not handle. This was a case where being too successful just didn't pay off. Curiously, many sisters share this same overprogrammed mentality, but it backfires in a different way. Instead of attracting loads of successful men, we find ourselves right smack in the middle of "no-man's-land." We spend years in school, trying to better ourselves and increase our station in life, and then find out that we have (unwittingly!) improved ourselves right out of the market.

How many times have we been with a group of women and the conversation turns to the subject of how hard it is to find a good man. The complaints have almost become like a mantra. Sisters say that all good men are either already taken, gay, in jail, or in interracial relationships. Things are never quite exactly what they seem. Of course, the same facts are true regarding trophy men.

Good men are, in fact, not so hard to find. By the late nineties, the majority of blacks age twenty-five and older were getting educated, and a sizeable percentage (14 percent) earned at least a bachelor's degree from college. As much as 16 percent of black men over the age of sixteen worked at what was considered "managerial and professional/specialty" jobs, like engineers, dentists, teachers, lawyers, and journalists. The black community is strong, with over eight million families; almost half include married couples, and more than half have the traditional two children in their family unit. And we believe in marriage, with 41 percent of black men and 37 percent of black women age fifteen and older being married.

The picture gets a little stickier for the black community when we consider homicide rates, incarceration, a higher rate of unemployment, and other ills of society that cause the numbers of truly eligible men to dwindle. (It only takes a rudimentary understanding of politics and the traditional social structure of our country to understand why things are as they are, but that's a whole different book.) But, according to the latest census statistics, 75,000 blacks age twenty-five and older have doctorates or professional degrees. Trophy men are definitely out there, but their numbers are somewhat limited. Change your attitude. Become an optimist. We may be forced to play the game with fewer players, but there is no doubt that trophy men exist. And surely each one needs a woman. Why shouldn't that woman be you?

One thing you should bear in mind while reading this book is that all of the women interviewed definitely had one thing in common—we were once standing in your exact shoes, as single women looking for a suitable mate. We all could recall the frogs we had to sift through before we got our prince, that walk of shame we took before we found our way to the hall of fame. Trophy men aren't easy to come by, but it is possible. The women you'll meet on the following pages are living proof of that.

SECRET #1:

Men Listen to What You Say, So Be Clear About What You Want

HAVE YOU EVER WANTED SOMETHING SO BAD THAT IT consumed all your energy? You thought you'd die without it, or just about pop because you were afraid you'd never get it? Then, finally, you got whatever it was that you were dying to have, and it was a letdown! All that craving and plotting and planning, and the moment comes, but you can't figure out why you feel so vacant, empty, and downright disappointed? You finally got the object of your desires, but everything fizzled instead of sizzled.

It happens all the time with silly things like expensive shoes, or designer purses with fancy initials all over them. But it can also occur with more significant things: the snazzy car that you're too paranoid to park on the street; the college degree that has nothing to do with your everyday job; the state-of-the-art exercise machine with clothes draped all over it. And as hard to believe as it may seem, the same thing can happen with a man. You may have spent a lot of time and effort in pursuit of a particular man and, once you were in the relationship, realized that he bored you to death. Or perhaps you realized that the relationship itself wasn't what you expected or wanted. How did that happen?

It's likely that you didn't have a clear sense of what you wanted. Many of us sheepishly go along with what other people want us to do, or what we thought was expected of us, or what some guy wanted (or didn't want), until we lose sight of what's meaningful to us.

Often, what we *think we want* in a partner is not *what we need.* A certain glossy image comes to mind, based on nonsense like movie-star looks, a nonstop romance, a calendar boy's body, and limitless credit cards. Single women spend countless hours in hot pursuit, chasing after the illusion, and once they get him, they realize he is just that: an illusion! If women are not careful, they can find themselves in a make-believe mess that is not what they wanted at all. They thought they had the trophy man, but instead they got the booby prize.

Many women have forgotten or become confused about what they want and need from a boyfriend or husband. Others have had such disappointing experiences with men that they actually begin to believe that the man who can meet their needs doesn't really exist. So they lower their standards as a pragmatic measure.

It is impossible to meet a man, date, or build a meaningful love affair if you don't know or have lost track of what you need in a mate. Truly understanding what really matters to you is the first step in conquering the confusion and disappointment you may often face in your love affairs.

So ask yourself this basic question: What do you truly want to gain from meeting men and dating? A majority of women will resoundingly answer that they want a meaningful relationship and ultimately a lifelong commitment. But is this really the case?

Early in life, when a woman is young and carefree, she dates men to satisfy momentary needs. Who can't remember a time in high school when a girl's most pressing criteria for choosing a man was his looks, how fast his car was, or how many points he scored to win the homecoming game? Girls go out with guys for fun. What woman among us doesn't look back at her boyfriends from years ago, chuckling in disbelief as she asks herself, "How did I ever go out with him?" How? Well, it didn't matter back then. Our romantic value system and goals were a lot different when we were just girls.

But you may be surprised to know how many women are still stuck in that pattern of chasing men for superficial qualities. It may no longer be if he can dunk a basketball, but the prestige of the company he works for, or the amount of money he received in his bonus check last year. These women aren't ready for commitment. They worry that they haven't played around enough, or that they will have to give up too much if they settle down. These women are just like many men: never satisfied with their love lives, always wondering if something much better is lurking right around the corner. We complain a lot about men who string us along. But many of us are just as guilty of this kind of immature behavior.

Don't mistake the message. There is absolutely nothing wrong with just having fun or hanging out, if that is what you really want. That's a period of life that you may have to live through. But there are a lot of women who chant this mantra of "just wanting to have fun" when deep down they know in their hearts that they truly want something more. We tell ourselves, "He might be the one," before our first big date with a new man, then find ourselves going to extremes to attract him, including buying outfits that look just right: sexy, slim, fashionable, feminine, and sometimes even "wifey." We sometimes starve ourselves to look thinner, mash our boobs into miracle bras, cut our hair, extend our hair, glue on our nails, change our makeup, put music on our stereo, and on, and on, and on . . .

all of this effort so that we can have "fun." Doesn't sound like fun.

When we become adult women, our values and priorities change. The fun of impressive cars, cute faces, and athletic achievements fades away, and we're left to decide upon a whole new set of priorities and values for ourselves and the men with whom we have relationships. Then we get stuck in another pattern—not admitting to ourselves or the people around us that we are ready for something real.

Take Courtney, for example. A thirty-five-year-old doctor, Courtney, spends countless hours week after week on elaborate dates that sound like something out of a movie. She and her man of the moment spend weekends on a private chartered fishing boat, having romantic dinners for two at the art-museum restaurant, or at bed-and-breakfast getaways complete with private cooking classes. We all have a girlfriend like Courtney. In fact, we envy her because she seems to have a dream life. While everybody else is sitting at home on the weekends, she's being wined and dined on expensive field trips for adults.

But don't be so quick to assume that she's got it made. Invariably, women like Courtney look up months (and quite often years) later, and wonder why other women have committed and even married, while she's still just hanging out. Courtney is dissatisfied with her love life (or will quickly realize that she's dissatisfied) because those fabulous dates never lead to anything meaningful. She'd love to get married and settle down one day. In fact, she's scared stiff of growing old alone. But her approach with men doesn't encourage commitment.

Like many single successful career women, Courtney says that she "just wants to have fun," and in saying so and behaving accordingly, she is her own worst enemy. She says she doesn't need a man, that she just wants to have a buddy for companionship, and that's just how her boyfriends see her. She's a great companion, full of fascinating ideas and entertainment, and she doesn't have to be taken too seriously. She's a party girl, demanding little more than a great time, and getting just that in return.

Contrast this with women who married trophy men. They expected not only companionship, but also commitment and growth in their relationships. They weren't intimidated or ashamed to admit that just having fun wasn't fun anymore. Many women make the mistake of thinking a man will be scared off if she is up-front about her intentions. Quite the contrary. Women set the course of a relationship.

Alice, a buyer for a large department store on the West Coast who is married to a stockbroker, explains:

> When I first met my husband, he did not quite know what to make of me. As a matter of fact, I remember it just like it was yesterday. We were having dinner, and he said something about how modern women mostly just want to have fun. I took him by surprise because I immediately, right then and there, told him that could not be further from the truth with me. I explained—as delicately as possible so I wouldn't scare him away, but firmly enough that he knew I wasn't just fooling around—that I was not just looking for a good time. I told him that, quite truthfully, if I took the time to go out and get to know a man, I had hopes and expectations that we could develop a friendship or perhaps even more (providing the match was right). Don't get me wrong, I didn't start telling him that I wanted to get married or what size wedding ring I wanted or what type of reception I wanted. All joking aside, I know that coming on too strong can be the kiss of death with a new relationship. But, on the other hand, I think that by letting Len know right off the bat that I was serious and looking for something serious, he knew which direction to take. It gave

him an exit if he didn't want to be bothered with establishing a serious relationship. In retrospect, I was a bit younger then and sure of myself. I think that being truthful and up-front was what really appealed to Len. He knew I was a serious sister. Something about this struck a positive chord with him, and it just blossomed from there. I never stopped to wonder what it would have been like had I played into the "girls just want to have fun" image. Had I done that, it might very well have been the beginning of the end. I learned my lesson earlier, much earlier, that if you act with a devil-may-care attitude, guys will treat you in a footloose and fancy-free manner.

If given the chance, most men will use women. If a man is comfortable in a relationship, he'll let it sputter along as long as he thinks he can get away with it. But a man is able to take advantage of a woman only if she allows him to do so. Women who married well showed men that they had self-respect and certain expectations for the relationship. They refused to let a man string them along, dilly-dallying forever. It's a tricky prospect to avoid coming across as too demanding, too calculating, or too one-track-minded. But if a woman presents herself as deserving and entitled to as much love and respect and hope as she's willing to give, she'll get it back in return. It can be a mighty thing when a woman realizes she has power over her relationships and control over what she wants and expects from men.

Dating is time-consuming and expensive. Be clear about what you hope to gain from it. One woman I interviewed made a very telling analogy. "You'd never to go college without declaring a major, and you'd never plan a fund-raiser without knowing who'd get the money. So why in the world would a grown woman spend serious time with a man without an endpoint in mind?

Don't date a man if you have no real reason to date him. Don't waste valuable time."

Not only did women who married trophy men admit to themselves and others that they were ready for a committed relationship that would lead to marriage, they also knew what qualities they wanted in a husband.

I know women who go into each and every relationship with a checklist or a wish list. It might seem cold, but it's not at all. It is simply realistic. Paula, who is married to an investment banker, explained it quite nicely. "You wouldn't just walk into a car showroom with the hopes and dreams of getting a car but without any idea of what you want. If you were naïve enough to simply let the salesman lead you around by the nose, you'd certainly end up with something you didn't want, couldn't afford, or couldn't stand to drive. Why would you approach things differently with something as important as a mate?" Paula is not cold and, in fact, she is not necessarily overly pragmatic. She doesn't mean to imply that finding a mate is as trivial as buying a car, but she has a good point.

When we make important life decisions, we usually have an idea in our head, or a working list from which we make comparisons, and draw conclusions. Consider, for a moment, your apartment, condo, or house. There are certain things that you prefer regarding location, the layout of the place, and the way it is decorated; certain things you dislike; and some things you absolutely cannot tolerate. Likewise, think of choosing a career or field. If you can't stand the sight of blood, you would no more consider going into medicine than someone who hated the thought of dealing with numbers would go into accounting. The same thing goes when sizing up men and deciding who might make the cut for your long-term goals.

When a woman hasn't set down her criteria for her life mate, her love life can seem like a runaway train. She'll confuse a man's good manners with affection, she'll mistake lust for love, Mr.

Wrong will start looking like Mr. Right. She'll lower her expectations and settle for far less than what she'd originally hoped for. She'll get tangled up in the absurdities of simply meeting men— any man—without sticking to the criteria she wanted for herself. And then she'll end up in an unhappy relationship, and it's the old fizzle instead of sizzle. Like all the fancy designer stuff you thought you had to own, the man you focused on getting wasn't the one you truly wanted or needed.

My good girlfriend Stephanie is quite simply a star in every aspect—Ivy League education, a law degree, and a prestigious job with an advertising firm. She is six feet tall in bare feet, thin as a rail, and has the looks of a runway model. And if that isn't enough, she is a really nice girl.

We met when she was twenty-seven, and amazingly, she had already gone through the trauma of a divorce from her first husband. Apparently, they had different goals in mind, and she could no longer "just go along to get along." Having children and starting a family was important to her, but her husband was adamantly against having a family. He didn't want to "limit himself." Finally, things came to a head, and because of their differences about having children, they divorced. Stephanie told me she would never again compromise or pretend that she did or didn't want something to get or keep a man. The next time she met a man and became involved with him, she was very up-front about letting him know what she wanted out of life. Luckily, he wanted the same things, and one thing led to another. It sounds too good to be true, but it happens all of the time. Quite often honesty with trophy men pays off.

Although none of the women interviewed literally kept a written list, I got the impression they walked into serious relationships knowing what they wanted and what they refused to compromise on. They knew what made a man marriage material. It might seem unfair or cold-hearted, but is there anything in life that is not judged acceptable versus unacceptable, better versus worse?

Certainly there are qualities that all women would want in their husbands. In speaking with countless women, both young and old, long married and newly wed, a clear picture of a good man emerged. It has *nothing* to do at all with looks, or money, or social status, or a bunch of highfalutin' degrees scribbled after his name. It has *everything* to do with the man as a person, and how he interacts with you.

What makes a man a good husband? He is loving and considerate; a true friend and companion. He is gainfully employed and financially secure, the kind of man who not only carries his own weight, but also takes very seriously the task of caring for his family when the need arises. He doesn't have to be drop-dead gorgeous and, in fact, is often ordinary looking, but he takes care to be well groomed and to pull himself together. He is the kind of guy with the clean smile, the timely conversation, the sensible clothes, and designs for his future. He may not be the most popular man in his set, but he certainly is open and receptive to meeting new people and forging new relationships.

But even though there are things we would all want in a husband, in some ways your criteria is still very unique. You know that expression, There is a lid for every pot? Trophy men are not one size fits all.

Let's take an example. Suppose you are sitting with your girlfriend at a trendy sidewalk café in the most exciting part of town. You've finished your meal and you are both sipping coffee when three men stroll by and, just by chance, are seated next to your table. The two of you take inventory, and this is what you see: One man has dreadlocks and a casual appearance; linen pants, sandals, and a backpack. He reminds the others he won't be able to make an appointment because he is taking his class on a bug safari in the park next weekend. The next fellow is an impeccable dresser; pinpoint-starched cotton shirt, pleated slacks, and the requisite cell phone that rings with an important-sounding call every ten minutes. He has a Palm Pilot and reminds the others about an important fund raiser that is coming up. The third guy is "everyman"; dressed in blue jeans and an alumni T-shirt, joking about the game on TV last night, his tennis racket tucked under his chair for a few sets after lunch. He is telling his friends about "a nice woman" he met last weekend and how he plans on calling her to ask her out.

They pay the bill and agree on meeting again, same time next week. After the threesome is well out of earshot, you turn and ask your girlfriend, "Wow, what a catch! Did you see him?"

Your girlfriend, practically drooling, answers, "Yeah. How come we can never catch a man like that?" You each rattle on about how appealing he seemed, how you would kill to have a boyfriend or husband like that, when the thought occurs to you—which man is she talking about?

This scenario underscores an important point; an ideal man for one woman might be a reject for another. The kind of man some women can only dream about may, in fact, be humdrum for others. A lot of factors come into play in determining why a certain woman chooses a certain man. For example, she might be at a particular junction of her life where looks, or education, or prestige, or money, or sex, or companionship and friendship mean more than anything else to her. On the other hand, she may be strongly motivated by what her friends and family think of her choice in a mate. Or perhaps she has put herself on a time schedule because her biological clock is ticking away. She has babies to birth, a mortgage to pay, and a retirement fund to build.

How do you go about developing your criteria? During the interview process with the various wives of trophy men, I detected a recurrent pattern: Women who married trophy men had compared their future husbands to the other men they knew.

By "the other men they knew," I mean women quite often either consciously or subconsciously compared serious boyfriends to their fathers, and even put great stock in their fathers' opinions of their boyfriends. Others looked to the male guidance figures and caregivers in their life, like their pastor, or special teachers who influenced them. Time and time again, women would recall how something about their special trophy man reminded them of their mentor, their professor, or someone who had made a positive imprint on their life.

Women, by nature, tend to make comparisons among their friends and acquaintances. Just think about the last big get-together or party you had with a group of sisters. The chances are pretty high that you can remember, at the very least, what somebody had on, how terrific their hair looked, that their stories about their vacation or work were mesmerizing, or that they had on the most gorgeous outfit you had ever seen. It's not necessarily a superficial thing; it's just that women compare and contrast their lives with others' as a way of assessing and improving their own. It is exactly the same with boyfriends and, quite often, husbands.

Women who were surrounded by friends who married, and married well, quite often expected the same thing for themselves. It's sort of a pack mentality—"if she can do it, I can do it too." There's also something very encouraging about seeing a best friend successfully land the man of her dreams. The most interesting of all were the women with truthful girlfriends who were able to tell them that there is more to relationships and marriage than just romance and love. Girlfriends who talk honestly with their friends about how difficult marriage can be and how much time and effort a successful marriage takes often give the kind of realistic advice that makes for a sensible and reality-based idea of the perfect man.

Having examples to follow, focusing on specific qualities,

and being realistic are very important when developing your list of criteria. There are women who have a list of desired qualities a mile long, and you know what? They are still spinning in circles. I loved Terry MacMillan's book *Waiting to Exhale,* as did millions of other women. The story struck a chord with so many women because MacMillan pointed out every single woman's dilemma. If you haven't read the book or seen the movie, there is one particularly funny scene where a girlfriend at the office has a sexual liaison with an affable dud. (This is the only nice way I can say it, girls.) He was a chubby, overeager lech with money and a great job, whom the woman forced herself to sleep with once or twice. The man, frustrated because he has so much to offer, asks the aloof girl, "What do you want?" She rattles off a fantasy list about a house, kids, and cars, and then says, "*I want it all.*" Although she is being honest, she is totally unrealistic. You can "want it all," but a woman has to prioritize and really choose what's most important and meaningful to her.

Consider keeping a working list in your mind of qualities that are important and meaningful to you. It's not about what your mother, sister, or your best friend wants in a man. This is about your needs.

Considerations for Your Mental Wish List

1. **Decide if looks are really important. What are you willing to compromise on? Does it bother you if he's skinny or fat? If he's shorter than you are, or if he is much, much taller? Remember that even the most handsome of men will age, sooner or later. Looks fade, but true character remains forever.**

2. How important is it that he have a successful career? Are you willing to hang in there until he gets his act together if he is in the early stages of his professional growth? Are you willing to hang in there if he has not yet gone to school or had the necessary training for his ultimate career goal? Are you willing to share in his dream of "hitting it big" in something sexy or glamorous and just off of the mainstream? Would you be willing to work at a day job while he develops his art studio, photography studio, recording studio, or writing lab?

3. How important is his intelligence? Some women find extremely brainy men appealing, while others find them just too nerdy.

4. Are you planning on having kids? If so, are you wondering about what type of characteristics your kids will inherit from their father?

5. Is his family background important to you? Some girls refuse to date a guy from "around the way," even if he has the best intentions and seems to be on the fast track for success. On the other hand, many women judge the man by his achievements and deeds, not by the neighborhood where he grew up or the high school he attended. A trophy man is often an everyday man: a police officer, a postal worker, a fireman, a contractor, or a man with his own small business. Wise women look at the total picture. It was very telling that sometimes the older and most prestigious trophy men were not born with

silver spoons in their mouths. Quite often, the guys who become self-made men and forge their own way in life are the most successful.

6. How important is it that he has money? Guys take issue all of the time with cold-hearted women who only want to use them for expensive gifts or dates and then drop them like hot potatoes. Be careful what you wish for, as quite often men with money to spare have loads of easily dispensable women. The majority of women married to trophy men controlled their own finances and achieved financial independence before they married. They didn't need a trophy man to give them money or buy things for them.

7. Are there some things you absolutely will not tolerate in a relationship? I have met sisters who would not go out with a military man because they simply did not want to move all over the country or make the sacrifices that military wives often have to make. Similarly, I have met women who have refused to date men who have ever been in an interracial relationship, claiming that it ruins and spoils them, as ridiculous as this may sound. Other women refuse to go out with a man who has any type of criminal record, which is not at all surprising.

8. How do you feel about somebody else's children? Other women refuse to even give a man the time of day if he already has children. It did not matter whether he was divorced with children or had children out of wedlock. Many women are afraid

of the long-term implications of dealing with some other woman's child for the rest of their lives.

9. Take careful note of a man's views on children and family. If he firmly resists the idea of raising a family, and children are something she hopes and dreams for, the strong-willed woman will simply walk away.

10. Are children in your plans at all? Many women *don't want children.* There is absolutely nothing wrong with opting out of the baby chase. Consequently, it's important that these women find men who aren't looking forward to fatherhood. These women value, and want, a good marriage—a solid foundation for a life with true companionship. They approach the idea of a marriage with the same undying tenacity and vigor as their "mommy-minded" counterparts, concentrating their energies on their man and marriage rather than children. They refuse to feel guilty because of their life choices, and why should they?

When you start thinking about these types of questions (and believe me, there are many, many more), you're developing a concrete sense of what you want in a mate. If you know what you want, you'll get what you want. That's true with most things in life. It's particularly true with marrying a trophy man.

SECRET #2:

Make Your Days as a Single Woman the Best Days of Your Life

WHILE INTERVIEWING WELL-MARRIED WOMEN, I BECAME aware that they all seemed grounded, with a firm grip on reality. They are aware of the fleeting nature of life, and appreciate the small joys of life, little blessings that bring wealth, and the importance of making and sticking to priorities. These were not women with pipe dreams. They did not chase unrealistic goals or folly. They spoke in terms of the here and now. They knew how to live for the moment, not in an impetuous way, but in an unassuming way that reminds them that nothing is promised or owed to them. After all, only a fool feels unrealistically entitled.

In living independently, the women who married well first forced themselves to get a life. They were able to entertain, support, and motivate themselves. They ignored the fear of attending social functions alone, realizing that if they didn't go by themselves, they might not ever go. They believed that their lives were what they made of them, and maximized their interests, hobbies, and social outlets when they didn't have boyfriends.

Jean is a retired school administrator who has been married for over fifty years. Although she might be a senior sister, her attitude is incredible and the advice she gives on marrying a trophy man is timeless. Back in her day, Jean was quite active in her sorority. She explains that it was quite uncommon for a black woman to travel alone as a young adult. But Jean was really what you would call hard core with her sorority, and attended all of its functions. It was something that she enjoyed and believed in. So much so, she was a founding member for graduate chapters in her area: She instituted charitable programs that are alive and well to this day, and she has been cited at several national conventions for her outstanding contributions to the community as a whole. Jean explained,

> When I first met Doug, I think it [my attachment to my sorority] kind of caught him off guard. I did not like my sorority, I loved my sorority. And I still do. Initially, he felt a little jealous because he thought I gave it more time than I gave him. But gradually, he began to see that it was an integral part of my life. It was something that I held dearly and a way in which I defined myself when I was a young woman. Once he understood exactly what it meant, and how much it meant to me, he started to try to understand and support me in all of my endeavors that were related to the sorority. For example, I can remember going to our regional meetings in Chicago, after I was engaged, and Doug would drive me down there. Later, once we were firmly on our feet and married, he even got a plane and would fly me back and forth to our conventions. This gave him a great deal of pride, and I felt like I was on top of the moon when my sisters heard that my husband was "flying me in" for the regional conferences and meetings. Although Doug was obviously not active, he seemed to somehow

appreciate me more because of my dedication and commitment to my sisters and our public-service programs.

When I first heard this story, I could barely believe it. This was a bona fide trophy man who was flying his own plane back and forth, thirty years ago. Jean and Douglas are not high rollers or flashy people, but his interest was in aviation and hers was in her sorority, so he made it his business to try to combine the two and make things work. Jean jokingly wonders whether or not things would have clicked so beautifully had she not had an interest that made Doug take notice.

In fact, many of the women who later married trophy men considered their single lives in some ways more intriguing, diverse, and productive. A particularly wise woman explained that once she accepted the fact that she might be single forever, she could "get on with the other business of life." She didn't look at being single as a death sentence, so it wasn't. Of course, she wanted love and she wanted a man. But she actively worked on her own personal happiness by dedicating her free time to herself. She stayed busy doing the things that made her happy, and her happiness led to personal growth and change.

It seems easy for these *now married* women to praise living single and reminisce about the good old days. But it was that period of life—the time spent making their own happiness alone—that 1) protected them from becoming involved with unsavory men, and 2) made them more appealing to trophy men.

Paige was an attractive, second-generation doctor who moved from a Midwest town to Dallas while she was in her late twenties. Dallas has a huge young professional Black population, and she thought her chances of meeting a trophy man there were much better than in her smaller Midwestern hometown. But despite her professional connections, her membership in an exclusive social club, and the perceived large number of men in Dallas, Paige remained single well into her thirties. That's when she began to panic.

When she finally met Peter, he seemed too good to be true. He seemed driven, and owned his own business. He was so busy, he didn't have time for friends. Peter was so successful that he was always between contracts and about to launch another major deal. The problem was, Paige could never quite explain exactly what his job was, what his business card meant, or why they didn't know any of the same people. But she was so wrapped up in him, she gave him keys to her condo and he'd practically moved in before she knew what hit her. Only then did she learn that everything was a complete lie. There were no contracts. No job. No nothing. Just a fraud. Paige didn't know any of his family and friends because he'd kept them a secret from her. It seems he didn't want her to find out about his criminal record. Only after a frightening breakup and a frantic rescue effort in the still of the night by her older brothers was Paige able to shake him and cover her tracks.

Women have to rely on their instincts. Paige sensed something was wrong about her boyfriend from the jumpstart, but she'd been too intoxicated with the idea of being in love to listen to the little nagging voices in her heart and head that warned her. Dallas had disappointed her, she felt like she was getting old, and she didn't want to admit that her move had been a total loss. So in her eagerness to find somebody, anybody, to love, she let her guard down. Because she'd been blinded by panic, this fraudulent man was able to slip into her life.

Many men, but particularly dangerous men, can detect frantic and desperate behavior. Successful men, on the other hand, avoid desperate women because they realize a frantic woman is not so much in pursuit of them, but in the pursuit of *any* man.

Trophy men are too busy with careers and life's challenges to rescue women who are looking for charity or miracle workers.

The women who married trophy men weren't looking for a man, or anybody for that matter, to save them or give them a new lease on life. Most men don't really want to save women—especially not the woman they will chose to become their wife. A truly independent woman will stand out every time. A woman alone can be brave. And bravery is sexy.

Most of the women I spoke to paid as much attention to their professional lives as their personal lives when they met their future husbands. They actively pursued their careers for four primary reasons: self-fulfillment, camaraderie and friendship, the intellectual challenge it provided, and money or economic stability. They didn't marry their trophy man for money. They didn't need to, because they had their own.

These women subscribed to *The Wall Street Journal*, *Money* magazine, *Morningstar* reports, or *Forbes*. Not only did reading these publications educate them about issues all working people should understand, it also gave them the opportunity to make informed decisions about their own money and participate in conversations about the market, money, and finance. Monica, a pharmaceutical rep, says she felt trophy men respected her because she was able to converse about the finances of the company she worked for. "A lot of men assumed that I would simply parrot what I'd learned about my product. But I went beyond that, to understand the growth and organizational structure of my company. When I was able to explain things and formulate my own ideas about finances, men sensed I wasn't just some fake." And on the flip side, once she understood the concepts of finance, earning power, and investment, Monica was able to easily discern which men were fakes and frauds. By simply talking with them, she could determine whether they were talking trash to try to impress her, or if they truly knew their stuff.

Perhaps these women weren't wealthy, but they were pursuing and achieving their goals. In that way, they were successful women. Successful men want successful women. That may seem obvious, but it is an often overlooked fact.

Gone are the days of "the little lady," a woman was sent to charm school and groomed to be the docile and supportive wife behind the successful husband. For one thing, being nothing more than a wife sets a dangerous precedent for women. Don't misunderstand; it's normal and fantastic even, for some sisters to surrender the workplace to be a wife and homemaker. However, if they do, then they should pursue this role just as aggressively as the hard-core "career girls" pursue theirs. *Whatever you do, give it your best!* Nobody, man or woman, should allow themselves to be easily replaced or dispensable. The women who marry trophy men know that their husband's success and prestige are just that—*his,* and not hers! Living though your man will eventually rob you of your self-worth and self-esteem.

Just look at the late Princess Diana of Wales. When she married the future king of England, the ultimate trophy man, she was a shy woman-child, seemingly content to exist for the sole purpose of pleasing her husband. But she soon tired of that empty existence and quite publicly let the people know about it. Fast-forward to a few messy infidelities later, and Diana had a divorce under her belt and a whole new attitude. Instead of looking older or bitter, she looked fresher and better. And best of all, because of her charity work, people loved her for herself, not because of who she married. She was most radiant when she moved from behind the shadow of her husband, and she'll be remembered as a glamorous role model who blossomed under her own direction. All of us should strive to be our own woman and have our own identity.

Having your own life means having strong preferences and desires. The women who married trophy men were very interesting, and interesting women attract interesting men. Whether they played tennis and golf in small local leagues, visited museums and attended live performances, crafted and sold their handiwork at local bazaars and galleries, or participated in discussion groups for literature and music appreciation, these were activities that they pursued seriously with the fervor of weekend experts.

They often belonged to sororities, charitable organizations, and professional organizations. Many of these groups were for women only, so they obviously didn't join to meet men. The female bonding in these groups was a source of strength and development for them. And they never downplayed or shortchanged their interests for the men they dated. They routinely set apart personal time, without their men, to pursue the interests that brought them joy. They did not set out to indoctrinate their romantic partners in their hobbies or interests, but many men were intrigued by those hobbies just the same.

Bonnie is a prime example. She is an accountant Monday through Friday, but she fancies herself an aficionado of African sculpture. She's taken weekend classes on the subject at the community college, owns and has completely read a small personal library dedicated to the art, and knows the African-art section of her local museum like she knows the back of her hand. When Bill, a successful real-estate entrepreneur, met Bonnie, he truly believed she was the most interesting and exotic woman he'd ever known. Bill was used to asking women what they wanted to do on a date and the women answering, "Whatever you want to do is okay with me." But Bonnie broke the mold. She always gave succinct answers on which restaurants she liked, which movies piqued her interests, and which social functions she considered a waste of her time. "I'm not one of those pushy, bitchy women who comes across like a little dictator, barking orders to her man. But I'm not a dizzy blonde who's eager to please, answering yes to whatever her man asks." She had her own tastes and preferences, and her very specific individuality came across as a real attribute to her trophy man. They went to an African-art exhibit on their first date, and they've been married for twelve years.

An older woman once had a quirky way of explaining the dating game to me: "Quality in, and quality out." At first I was not sure what she was talking about, but she explained that the phrase implies that what a woman attracts, often mirrors the image she herself portrays. We all know women (perhaps even ourselves) who decide they are finally ready for serious love—to settle down and marry—but feel as though all the good ones have been taken. Although some things are out of our control, in this case, what is seemingly impossible is very possible. A lot of it depends on the message that you put out there and the image you portray.

By making your single days the best days of your life, you are being deliberate about the direction in which your life should go. If you use the time to develop all of your best qualities, you'll not only be a happier person, you will also be well qualified for a quality mate.

SECRET #3:

Nurture Your Spiritual Center

A COMMON THREAD BINDING WELL-MARRIED WOMEN WAS that they often had an ongoing and meaningful relationship with God, and a faith that they deeply cherished. A woman's spirituality is not measured by things like regular attendance in church or being seen consistently in the front pew. These women considered themselves believers and, when closely questioned, felt that God gave them hope and meaning in *all aspects* of their lives. Having something to believe in gave them strength, made them complete, and allowed them to make fundamentally moral decisions with a grasp of what was right and wrong.

The women I interviewed realize that being in touch with themselves spiritually made them stronger, better, and more resilient women. As Alma, a telecommunications representative, once said during an interview, "If you have something to believe in, something to hold on to, it is a lot harder to lie to yourself. Having a conscience means that you sleep well at night, it means you don't walk over people or use them for your own benefit. When you come to terms with what you believe, you have to come to terms with yourself. This is the type of thing a man, especially an astute man or what you call a 'trophy man,' can see right away." Again and again, it was explained to me that taking time to know your beliefs and to strengthen your relationship with God inevitably meant that you get to know, really know, yourself as a woman.

Kelly, an elementary-school teacher, strongly believes that prayer, patience, and asking tough questions of herself gave her the strength to break off a long relationship with a man who was no good for her. "It's hard to accept that sometimes the man who you *really* want is not the man you *need*. I'd gotten so tangled up with this guy, I tried to ignore his heavy drinking, his three divorces, and his tendency to criticize. He made me miserable, but in my mind, I had to have him. Then I started thinking really hard about myself, my pride, and why I was stuck in a relationship that didn't make me happy. I started praying, not only at night, but also during work, in the shower, and at quiet moments at my desk. I started going to church and actually listening for a message. I tried to help myself. And I finally left him." A free woman, Kelly later met the man she'd marry.

The most spiritual of the sisters I spoke with did not rely on organized religion as much as they treasured their personal and spiritual beliefs. They did not believe in God because of piety, guilt, or pressure from others, but rather because of a need for guidance from a higher power. For example, nearly all belong to a church or denominational place of worship, but most admitted their attendance was sometimes sporadic and, occasionally, even shaky. But who was counting? Most of them truly believed that what they felt in their hearts was more important than their public actions.

Interestingly, women attended church or worship services most often when things were either going very well or very badly. The women agreed that the very acts of hearing sermons, communally praying, receiving sacraments, and singing spiritual music made them feel grateful in happy times and comforted them during the bad times.

Attending church service provided an opportunity for introspection and healing. Customarily, when they did attend church services it was usually alone, so that too much socializing would not distract them. Valerie explained things nicely. "It sounds obvious, but the times when I have been really low—problems at work, breaking up with a boyfriend, or not feeling good about myself, I went to church. If I was ashamed of something I had done, I would go to church and it really helped me." Time and time again, women gave me examples of attending worship services when they felt vulnerable. If they had just moved to a new city, they would duck in somewhere as a visitor; if they were out of town, they would possibly tune in to a television service or simply read from a prayer book; and finally, if they needed a bit of inner strength, they would sometimes just pray quietly in a stolen moment.

None of the women recommended church as a means to meet men. Of course, there's something very positive to be said about meeting a man at the social coffee hour after service. The mood is upbeat and hopeful, the dress proud and tasteful, and the idea of guttural sex is the last thing on his mind. But despite all of the positive reasons for meeting men at church, these women looked to worship service for much more. Using church to meet men or see their boyfriends would have somehow lessened the importance of the services.

The sisters with whom I spoke, who married trophy men, were not at all embarrassed at speaking about their spirituality or religion. These women had allowed their future husbands to see this spiritual side of them. If they were going to worship services, they were up-front about it with the man they were dating. They had Bibles in their homes and left them in plain sight. The Bibles weren't showcased, but they were not hidden away either.

Many believed it was their religious conscience that set them apart from the other women their trophy men dated. Because these women held themselves to a higher standard, and had a moral compass that kept them out of dangerous or debasing situations, the men they dated felt comfortable about considering them marriage material. A trophy man trusts that his future wife (and possibly the future mother of his children) is moral.

Believe it or not, there are women who are nervous about how their spiritual devotion will appear to the men they are dating and so downplay their religious commitments because of a man. They nearly always regret it. Let's take Linda, for example. Linda was raised in a strong Southern family and attended Sunday school and church for as long as she could remember. Sundays were special days, set aside in her childhood as a time for going to church, praying with the family, and then having Sunday dinner and meaningful conversation. But when she left the South and moved to the East Coast for a new job, she felt that this fundamental faith somehow did not jibe with being sophisticated. So, when she met Derek, she downplayed her religious beliefs.

I was so crazy about him, and I wanted him to think I was savvy and sophisticated. I can't believe I was actually dumb enough to disparage church and my religious upbringing just to make him think I was worldly. Somehow, when we first met, we got on the topic of religion, and I stuck out my neck and started talking about doubt and what religious men call "literalism." In other words, I told him I had serious problems with the idea that all men literally descended from Adam and Eve, that there was a great flood, you know, stuff like that. I thought it was sophisticated to have doubts. When I really think about it, I did and still do believe all of those things, but for some silly reason, I thought that being doubtful would make me mysterious and worldly in his eyes. It only came back to haunt me. In fact, I can remember hearing some things on the radio by Take Six and some other contemporary spiritual singers. Derek sounded off and began to criticize them— calling them "country," joking about how "churchgoers are the biggest hypocrites in the world," talking about all kinds of strange and unfamiliar things like deities and totally foreign religious beliefs. He thought I would agree and play right along with it, but I didn't. It's not to say that I judged other religions, but it just seemed kind of odd and creepy the way he lumped my belief (in Jesus Christ) with other deities that had nothing to do with Christianity. It really left a lump in my craw. I think that was a turning point when I went home and felt really ashamed that I had ever downplayed my beliefs to him. The fact that he practically badmouthed Christianity really did turn me off. I regretted that I hadn't been more of a woman and told him how I felt, and I regretted that I'd made the dire mistake, in the first place, of downplaying my own beliefs.

In many ways religion provides a moral compass for women. It is hard to misbehave or act up when you have a conscience. It is hard to be dirty when you are inwardly sensible or are afraid of the consequences. Believing in God, or something bigger than yourself, gives a sense of morality, and morality is how a woman determines the difference between right and wrong.

One woman was reluctant to give me specific examples of spirituality as it relates to relationships, explaining there was something taboo about discussing intimacy or sex and religion in the same context. What has sex got to do with it? As she explained it, "I knew lots of women who had absolutely no problem meeting a guy and then falling into bed with him. Some would bang him even after they had gone out just one or two times. Others would even give a guy oral sex. I wouldn't feel right about it; I couldn't imagine some guy on top of me or, heaven forbid, my mouth on him if I barely knew him. I'd feel too guilty—*dirty*, even. He could be some sleaze or psycho, and I just couldn't live like that." This woman understood an important point. Loose or irresponsible behavior is a lot less likely to happen if you have a conscience. After all, the universal theme in religion is right versus wrong, good versus bad, doing the right thing versus "just getting by."

There was something comforting in interviewing women who considered faith a sort of lifeline. They repeatedly used the term "something to hold on to" when describing their beliefs. Faith gave them strength. In fact, I was surprised to hear that a few still considered some of the old religious teachings timely. Said Karen, "People think the Bible is old-fashioned and out of date. But if you take time to review it, there are more stories in there that relate to current problems than you can imagine. There are lessons about illegitimate birth, women being judged and being treated unfairly, women with infertility problems, and husbands fooling around on their women. It shows that everything old is new."

It's important to point out that not all of the women I interviewed were Christians. In fact, one extremely fascinating sister from New Jersey adopted the Muslim faith in early adulthood. She later moved to the Caribbean and married a Muslim man. What strengthened the marriage and family she and her trophy man built was that they shared a common faith and belief system. They had similar hopes and dreams and values.

Whether Muslim or Christian or practicing any other religion, many trophy wives realize that some of the old laws and ancient teachings—things about women obeying their husbands and essentially being like property—are ludicrous for the modern woman. One respondent said, "Abraham owned slaves, right? But that doesn't very well mean it's okay to own slaves, does it?" We have to apply the stories to our lives and understand what they mean to us personally. Those that deal with regret, mistakes, and suffering are universal. That is where we can learn from religious writings.

On the other hand, women who married trophy men were very careful not to appear too pious. Sheila told me, "Nobody, man or woman, likes a goody-two-shoes or a holy roller. It's a turn-off." They didn't try to influence or convert a man early in their relationships. They avoided public proselytizing, judging others openly for their beliefs, or publicly praying. For example, they considered it bad taste to publicly pray over their food, or make the sign of the cross in mixed company before a meal. But when they witnessed a car accident or traumatic event, they more than likely prayed openly or evoked some religious supplication (i.e., "Dear God, I hope they're all right"). These public displays of belief were often quick, reflexive, and genuine, almost like a knee-jerk reaction, but *not* to impress others.

Sisters married to trophy men are not static. They are constantly growing, constantly reaching higher and striving for better. They can pinpoint pivotal times in their lives when they had to make choices—for example, whether or not to go to college or to continue college; whether or not to continue or postpone a pregnancy; whether or not to go to graduate school or take a job; whether or not to take a job offer near home or to move far away; or whether or not to break it off with a boyfriend or try to work it out—and through those choices their lives unfolded and grew. At each turning point, the majority of these women prayed, pondered, and considered their faith in making important choices. They felt their beliefs allowed them to be brave enough to venture out, make life-altering choices, and grow.

Although many did believe in coincidence and the concept

of faith, most believed that their individual actions had the greatest effect on the outcome of their lives. None believed in pure luck or destiny. These women, instead, believed individual choices and behavior had the greatest impact on the stories of their lives. As one put it, "You can have the chance of a lifetime in your hands, and make the choice to let it slip through your fingers."

Women married to trophy men, although having strong religious convictions, did not necessarily impose their personal religious beliefs on their men. Of course, they hoped for and worked toward a spiritual connection with their mate, but they avoided seeming pious or pushy with their men, or automatically assuming that what they believed, he would believe also.

Not surprisingly, many of these women recall that the major turning point in their relationships with their husbands was when they showed interest in or asked to share in more of their spiritual side. Some remember their trophy man suggesting he join her one Sunday at church, or asking if he could come to a class or workshop regarding Eastern versus Western religion. One woman explained, "When I was dating my husband, I knew we were serious when he started asking me what Presbyterians were; what we believe, how we were different. It showed interest and respect. He knew it meant something to me and in caring enough to learn about my beliefs, he cared enough to learn more about me, as a person."

It's very interesting that although trophy men visited their girlfriend's church, they did not necessarily join, even after marriage. Their commitment to *respect* their woman's beliefs did not necessarily mean a commitment to *adopt* her beliefs. And, likewise, these women did not expect or demand their husbands to assume their personal religion. I have found that interdenominational marriages were just as common as same denominational marriages.

Finally, it bears mentioning that these women noticed a difference between the men they simply dated and the man they ultimately married. Those who were *not* marriage material didn't take time to learn what was spiritually important to these women. It could be said that *they didn't distinguish the significant stuff, so they themselves became insignificant.*

SECRET #4:

You Don't Need to Look Far to Find Him

THERE'S AN AGE-OLD SAYING, "WHEREVER YOU GO...THERE you are." Women who've married well realize that geography and demographics make a difference only to a certain degree. If you have problems and excess baggage, you're likely to haul it around with you wherever you go. How many women make that move to Los Angeles, New York, Atlanta, D.C., Dallas, or Philly only to learn (the hard way) that large, densely populated cities can be the most lonely and unfulfilling places in the world, especially if you're unfocused, don't know what you want from life, and have no plan? Sure big cities have more men, but they also have more sleazeballs and losers looking to latch on to lonely women. Any city, any job, and any neighborhood is only what you make of it.

Some well-married women were in the same cliques as their trophy men. They often belonged to the same social circles. They went to the same schools. Their families shared the same fraternities and sororities, the same alma maters, and the same churches. As children, they were members of the same sports leagues. They'd shared legacies of Jack and Jill and similar groups for kiddies, and their moms served on the same charitable organizations like the Links, the North Easterners, and the Junior League. Increased exposure leads to increased odds of meeting the right man. It's easy to be in the right places at the right times if your family and people watching out for you have guided you there.

Of course, we enjoy a society full of possibilities, and "rags-to-riches" and "riches-to-rags" stories happen all the time. Many of these few privileged women, born lucky and marrying well, were shrewd enough to understand that they couldn't rely on their social standing alone to get them over. The inner circle that keeps successful people together is increasingly fluid, with both men and women moving in and out of it all the time. A woman lucky enough to be born with a silver spoon in her mouth can't afford to forget that she could easily lose it. Any woman who's born with ambition, desires, or smarts should believe she could penetrate that inner circle.

Hearing our subjects recall the specific logistics of when and where they met their husbands was like exploring a sunken treasure. Some women gave quite ordinary and mundane stories, while others slowly revealed an almost calculated approach to how they'd met their husbands.

After I took time to really comb through the fine details of the interviews and conversations with my girlfriends who'd married well, I was impressed—perhaps much more than I had expected—by the fact that many met their future husbands while in school. I want to be careful here. I am *not* implying that for a man to be successful he has to have gone to college, but the reality for many successful black men (in this day and age) is that most of them have had some type of advanced education or highly specialized training in their career field.

This is a touchy proposal. On the one hand, if you decide to go to college, you are at a young, footloose, and fancy-free time of your life. Those first few years out of high school are quite possibly dedicated to having fun and spreading your wings. The last thing on your mind is meeting a husband or settling down in a serious relationship. On the other hand, it was during their college lives that many trophy women met their husbands and began the business of forming serious relationships. I suppose the role is, as one sister explained, "When you're in college, have fun, but don't have too much fun." There used to be a goofy old saying that when you go to college you should get your degree, your *MRS.* degree. Although I would be hard-pressed to say that women in this day and age go to college specifically to find a husband, it would be ridiculous not to point out that college or secondary school (in the broadest sense of the term) or any type of professional training or education provide a fertile field for meeting young, ambitious men.

Many women, of course, don't meet the right man during the time they are in school. The older you get, the more clearly you understand that four years flash by in the blink of an eye. Quite often, women graduate from college not having met any men that they could even bear to spend more than a few weeks with—let alone build a lifetime and marriage with. Sure enough, these usually were the women who met their trophy man at places like private parties, social gatherings, conventions, and specific-interest festivals.

But consider for a moment that a woman might graduate from college and later go to a college reunion or alumni association gathering, and find out that some of the skinny little nerds have blossomed and become delectable and mature trophy men. I have talked with a lot of women who say they kept their lines of communication open well after graduating from school or moving on from their first job. Things like yearly Christmas cards serve a purpose. Even if they are only sent out to a handful of friends and acquaintances, they can help you keep in touch with the grapevine. People know how to get in touch with you, and it is easier to keep up with who has moved or been transferred to your city, who is recently divorced (it is a harsh example, but pragmatic and true), or who is really doing well in his career but may have not yet met the right woman.

Another plain truth is that many sisters are just not academically inclined. Some start college but never finish, while others just don't have the interest, dedication, or aptitude for a formal college education. If this is indeed the case, she can look to other venues for meeting trophy men. What do I mean by this? Everyone has an interest. If your interest is travel, join a travel group. Although your trophy man may not be a part of the group, you would be surprised what avenues are opened by simply networking with people who share a common interest. What if your interest lies in arts and crafts? It is not uncommon for cities and even larger towns to have craft guilds, art clubs, and continuing-education programs. Again, you just might meet an interesting fellow through these pathways. And if you don't, you might meet someone who has a friend who is open, available, and receptive. The list could go on and on; women interested in music could join music classes at their local community college, or sign up for season passes to the repertory theater or concert hall in their city. Women who are particularly athletic might want to join a coeducational soccer league, a swimming league, or tennis league.

It may not be easy, but if you sit down and, in a methodical way, decide what it is that interests you, the chances are pretty high that you will have fun simply by becoming active and pursuing your interest, and who knows, you might just meet the right man along the way.

A tried-and-true avenue for meeting trophy men is to ask friends (both male and female) to fix you up on blind dates with "nice guys." Who among us has not been fixed up on a blind date? The very *mention* of a blind date puts some women on edge in the same way that scraping fingernails across a chalkboard might. Yikes! However, it can be done and quite often leads to a happy ending. If you have treasured and trusted friends—for example, old college roommates or women you have grown up with—who know your background and your personality, they might be a worthwhile source of trophy men. Old and established friends generally share similar backgrounds, job experience, and social ranking. Consequently, it makes sense that they might have other "friends of friends" who share a lot in common with you. If you are honest with your friends and tell them that you would like to meet nice guys who are looking to meet a nice woman, you just might be surprised. It is important to go in without being too judgmental, but with your eyes fully open. Chances are pretty good that he will expect you to be a "dud" because you have to be set up by friends. Similarly, you might assume something is wrong with him, since his friends had to fix him up with you. But let's be serious after all; if both of you are open, willing, and receptive to the blind date, he will be just as hopeful as you are that things just might turn out for the best.

Commonly Named Places
Where Women Met Their Husbands
(Not necessarily listed in the order of frequency)

1. At a party sponsored by an organization or group, such as a fraternity, professional association, or volunteer group

2. At a party hosted privately at a friend's home

3. Through a mutual friend (for example, through blind dates, group outings, or family get-togethers)

4. While on vacation at high-end, inclusive-type resorts, interest-geared destinations, and conventions

5. At upscale, trendy, coed exercise clubs and exercise classes

6. In a class or interest group (for example, in sports lessons, language lessons, or community-based continuing-education classes)

7. While attending work-related conventions

8. At receptions, openings, and music festivals (such as jazz festivals, Black-art shows, and community theater)

9. In college or in graduate school

Asking married sisters *exactly where* they met their trophymen husbands was a real eye-opener. People are willing to discuss their stories, especially if they have a happy ending. The most common meeting ground was at school, or at parties. Some of the parties were private affairs given by mutual friends, while others were public functions thrown by sororities, fraternities, or fundraisers. Several women met trophy men at private cocktail parties, receptions, and at parties sponsored by their professional work-related organizations. Occasionally the parties were big, fancy deals, meaning holiday balls or formals, debutante balls, and formal dinner dances hosted by groups like One Hundred Black Men, the Links, and traditional Greek organizations.

It was surprising how many women mentioned an obvious fertile field for meeting men: weddings, wedding receptions, or through being members of the bridal party. These women fondly remembered everybody in attendance being "in a romantic mood, full of champagne, and seeing the world through rose-colored glasses." Other sisters met men when visiting churches, at the coffee klatch afterward, at choir practice, or at multidenominational get-togethers and outreach programs involving more than one congregation.

Others met the man of their dreams because he was their neighbor! Some connected and "started something" at the library (their public library, the medical-school library, the law-school library, or the business-school library). Others connected while working out in the gym, or having lunch at the company cafeteria, or while attending holiday block parties, or at public viewings of Black film and theater, or while attending barbeques for political candidates.

Some sisters (the artsy kind) got out there and found men at the big jazz festivals, at launch parties for trendy new black restaurants and clubs, or at classes in the community for subjects like photography, wine tasting, gourmet cooking, or mastering a foreign language. One woman met her trophy man at an auction for high-end oriental pieces and antiques. Another fondly remembers locking eyes at a writers' conference.

Some of the more athletic women often meet men while pursuing their love of exercise. Some met Mr. Right at tennis lessons, at the golf club, or at the gym. Some took coeducational classes for lessons in a sport they loved but had never had the chance to master. Others met trophy men while taking scuba lessons in the Caribbean. Wow! Some nabbed their dream boy at the National Brotherhood of Skiers, and the Black Enterprise/ Pepsi Golf and Tennis challenge.

The "busy bee" sisters met their men while they were on the run. Although the unusual and exotic examples were the exception, rather than the rule, it just goes to show that the trophy man might show up when you least expect him! I heard some serious Cinderella stories of women meeting men at friends-of-the-art-museum receptions, while kicking off the opening of a new acquisition. Another met the love of her life at a Congressional Black Caucus gathering. Another princess met her prince at a thank-you reception honoring celebrities and sports figures who'd volunteered time for a charitable organization. Some career-minded sisters met their trophy men at work, or at work-related functions. And it didn't always have to be in a dramatic and elite setting, either; many met in the company cafeteria or lunchroom, and some while jogging around the company parking lot. Another woman was seated next to her future trophy man on a coast-to-coast flight during a business trip.

Private parties are an ideal place to meet men. Dangerous, unsavory, and unwanted men have been screened out—at least more so than at a public bar or dance club. Of course, you can meet a loser or a fool at a private party too, but at least you have a small measure of insurance in knowing you can inquire about a person through a friend.

If you haven't been invited to any parties, don't despair. Simply throw your own party! Don't know that many single men? Give a "Six Degrees of Separation" party. Invite three men and three women. Have each woman invite six of her girlfriends and each guy invite six of his buddies. Already, that is a base of more than thirty people. Spice it up by stipulating that the guests must be the most interesting people they know. If you don't know six, then play around with the numbers. Money need not be a concern, because you can make it a potluck, or supply pizza and light snacks, and buy a box of wine and a keg for the bar. Keep it simple, dim the lights, then put some good tunes on the stereo, and you've got the potential for a fabulous party.

Here are some other ideas for meeting trophy men.

1. Be a "sport." Sports are a magnet for many men. If you aren't athletic-minded, start trying. If at all possible, buy season tickets, or tickets to as many home games as you can afford.

2. Join an organization. Join a civic-minded group or become closely affiliated with one. By "civic," I mean a group dedicated to charitable causes and improving the community. Some are quite selective and difficult to join. In fact, members don't join. They are invited. But relax. If you aren't targeted for membership, you can befriend a member, express your interest in attending the group's functions, and watch with interest when their sons, nephews, and friends turn out. If you're not sure where to start, check with the human relations department at your job; public galleries, museums, gardens, or zoos; the local humane society; the public relations director of local walk-a-thons or telethons in your city; any local radio stations; or national public radio or television stations. Tell them you're interested in volunteering, and ask if they have any groups of which you could become a member. Remember to stress that you'd like to join a group, otherwise you might end up working alone for free and not meeting anybody.

3. Shop till you drop. Go on a shopping spree. Identify the upscale department and specialty stores in your area, then hone in on the men's department. Dress and look your best, and assure all the salesmen and customers that you're shopping for your uncle, dad, or godfather. Accept any help, suggestions, and kind advice that comes your way, and see where it leads. Resist buying, unless it's just a simple tie or shirt that you can later use as a gift.

4. Get domestic. It's a cliché, but you can meet men in the grocery store. Frequent the upscale grocery stores and gourmet shops in neighborhoods located closest to large companies, firms, hospitals, universities, and younger, yuppie-type neighborhoods or subdivisions. Stop by after work when guys are swinging through to pick up their dinner from the deli section.

5. Sip a cup of java. Coffee and cappuccino joints attract a fun, upbeat, and savvy crowd. Go alone, take the newspaper, look your casual best, and pick a conspicuous table.

6. Go to a tried-and-true happy hour. Attend Friday happy hour in the nicest, most expensive, and upscale club or restaurant bar you can afford. Don't go for the cheapie all-you-can-drink joints, because they attract a cheap and boisterous crowd. Try not to go alone. Instead, go with girlfriends and firmly plan on leaving before it gets too late or too dark. Don't let yourself be seen drinking anything stronger than a glass of white wine. And nobody looks good with a cigar hanging out of her mouth (no matter how trendy), unless she's a movie star. There is always the risk of meeting lounge lizards at happy hour, but expensive places generally attract more of a professional crowd, and a few nice men do slip through.

7. Register for a summit. Scour special-interest magazines for announcements about jazz festi-

vals, ski summits, tennis summits, and golf summits. Although expensive, they attract an incredible crowd. If you don't get the magazines, ask your local librarian to help you find the information, or surf the Internet. Don't worry if you don't know much about jazz or the various sports because there are often clinics at the events to teach you. Even if you don't meet your trophy man, you'll have a load of fun and might get hooked on a yearly tradition!

8. Fly first class. When traveling, try to fly first class. The first-class section is a businessman's heaven. With some finagling with discount brokers and cheap-ticket outlets, you can sometimes buy first-class tickets for not too much more than full coach fare. You may also be able to cash in on frequent-flyer miles and trade miles for an upgrade.

9. Study the grapes. Enroll in a wine-tasting class. Check local gourmet shops or your community college. These classes are often well attended by older or more successful men, not your typical beer guzzler. You'll meet interesting people and learn something in the process.

10. Get politically correct. Attend a political rally. You'll meet concerned, active, and aware men.

11. Visit a bookstore. Check out one of the new mega-bookstores. They have books to interest everybody. Best of all, they encourage shoppers

to settle down in the aisle or the cappuccino bar and browse through the books or CDs of their choice. You should also attend author readings and signings, particularly for authors of business, sports, and science-fiction books, which attract a number of men. Sit in plain view, and you might just generate welcome attention. If you don't meet anybody, treat yourself to a self-help book, a classic you've always wanted to read, or one of the new best-sellers that interests you. It's a no-lose situation.

12. Make a bid. Attend the preview of an auction. There's no need to buy anything if you don't want to. All major cities have auction houses, where it's fun to see the style and value of different art objects, antiques, and furniture. While you're browsing, you might just meet somebody. Art and antiques fairs often attract single guys trying to decorate their bachelor pads. It's a small and eclectic group, but if you frequent the circuit, you'll be surprised at the trophy men you meet.

13. Get conventional. Official organizations exist in unlimited numbers. There are associations for engineers, nurses, lawyers, doctors, teachers, small businessmen, and entrepreneurs, just to name a few. Join an organization of your chosen profession and participate fully in its activities. Keep up-to-date by taking continuing-education classes related to your career or the career you're thinking about pursuing. It will make you a better person, but self-improvement aside, profes-

sional meetings and conventions are heavily attended by men—especially trophy men. Go with an open mind, and a smiling, receptive attitude, and you'll have a good chance of meeting a trophy man. If you don't belong to a profession (or if you do, but dare not surround yourself with the same kind of guys and colleagues who would bore you to tears!), then kick up your heels at the conventions open to everyone, but dedicated to the pursuit of serious fun. Has anyone heard of the jazz festivals? Or how about the aforementioned Ski Summit, or Golf Challenge? Make no mistake; these are selective venues, because they require money and planning for attendance. They're not the type of activities that "thugs" would enjoy, or willingly pay the entrance fee to attend.

14. Start "living right." Joining a church is a win-win situation. Of course, if you join only to meet men, you've completely missed the whole point. On the other hand, if you begin to nurture positive change and spiritual growth in your life, you open the door for a lifetime of possibilities. If a trophy man is sitting in the pew right in front of you, don't ignore him because you're meeting him at church. It just might be that God placed him there for you to find him.

15. Join a selective health club. Joining a health club also provides multiple benefits. Making a financial commitment to working out and exercising quite often means you are more likely to do it

than if you simply go out to jog in your neighborhood or do a few sit-ups in front of the television while Oprah is on. One girlfriend explained, "If I paid good money to belong to a health club, you can believe I would go regularly and exercise. I would hate to think of wasting all of that money for nothing." When I say "health club," I don't mean just any health club. We have all seen the type that makes you wrinkle your nose—the sweaty, stinky, muscleman's gym where there is nothing but heavy free weights, dark walls covered with mirrors, and weird-looking guys with little heads and big bodies who do nothing but lift weights and then look at themselves in the mirror. You can smell them a mile away and, as offensive as they are to you, *they don't want you there either.* These are not the kind of places where you bounce in, fully made-up in your matching pink leotard, and announce "Hi, guys." There are new coeducational clubs, usually the ones that are quite expensive and in nice neighborhoods, that cater to a young working crowd. You've seen the kind, with the juice bar and organic snack bar in the middle of the club, playing soft jazz or an urban hip-hop beat for you to work out to. They are the kind of places that have Pilates classes, step classes, and spinning classes. The people here take exercise seriously, but there is time to mingle and chat during your workout. Don't bristle at the high admission fee. Places like this generally charge an admission fee and a steep yearly membership charge so that they can maintain quality and cater to a selective clientele. They do this for a reason—just like country clubs, where they maintain high charges to keep out undesirables. Look at it as a social investment. If you figure out the cost per day for a year, ask yourself if it is worth that certain number of dollars a day to not only get healthy and exercise, but possibly meet new friends whom you would otherwise never be exposed to.

Socializing Solo: Good or Bad?

Putting yourself in the position to meet men means venturing out to the places where you can find them. Going to clubs, meetings, and social functions increases your odds, but it's not as easy as it sounds. First, as a woman you've got to look your best and act the part, not to mention psych yourself into the necessary frame of mind to play the dating game. But perhaps the most important step in getting out there is figuring out how and when you're going to go, and whether you're going alone or with a girlfriend.

Deciding if you should attend social functions alone, with a girlfriend, or with a pack of friends isn't as easy as it sounds. It's a decision that leaves open a multitude of potential pitfalls, and there are no simple solutions.

Men are more likely to approach you if you're alone. They will assume that you're either single, or in a single "frame of mind" if you attend a function alone. Second, men are afraid of rejection, especially in full view of a woman's girlfriends. Waltzing across a crowded room or dance floor to say hello and strike up a conversation is a lot easier when you're not surrounded by the peanut gallery, whispering and giggling about you and your every move. Nothing is more potent or volatile than a pack of women, cackling, drinking, gossiping, and laughing. It takes an extremely brave (or crazy) man to approach a tightly knit group of girl-friends with the intent of singling out just one. Most men avoid intimidating situations, and infiltrating a large group of women is often just too risky to try.

You also have a better chance of striking up a genuine one-on-one conversation if you are not shoulder to shoulder with a pack of girlfriends. Getting to know somebody through an initial conversation is difficult enough. Trying to have such a conversa-tion with a horde of buddies hovering around only makes it harder. When two people have a moment of privacy, complete with eye contact (instead of performing for the crowd), they have the opportunity to really see what the other person is like. Noth-ing can take the place of one-on-one conversation when you're getting to know somebody. If you *are* alone, you will receive more personal attention. Single women are more likely to be bought drinks, escorted to their car, even escorted home. A true gentle-man, if interested, will seize the opportunity to behave gallantly. There's something heartwarming about the attention, and a receptive woman will feel comfortable with it, and let the man know she appreciates the attention. It could be a great start to a relationship.

Many sisters are quite intimidated by—in fact, scared to death of—going out in a public place by themselves. It's not uncommon for a woman never to have eaten alone, gone to a movie alone, or attended a social function without a date. If you have not yet met a trophy man or someone whom you want to seriously date or establish a relationship with, this can be a diffi-cult situation. What's a woman to do? I was impressed by the fact that many of the sisters I spoke with knew the difference between *loneliness* and *solitude.* It's one thing to be lonely and holed up in a quiet apartment by yourself, but it's an entirely different thing to go out solo or enjoy your personal private time, either at home or out and about in public.

For women who are lonely (and it is nothing to be ashamed of, it can happen to any of us) it's a daunting task to get up and go to a club to meet people. We all know what kind of lounge lizards and sociopaths a woman can pick up at a club. But wise women advise us that it's terribly difficult, in fact, almost impossible, to meet anyone by simply sitting around at home. Events don't just fall out of the sky, and invitations don't just show up at your door complete with single men eager and willing to meet you. You have to go after what you want, and how can you know what you want if you are too scared to venture out into your community for events and social functions and give yourself a chance?

Much of the fear in venturing out alone is in our minds. One woman had no problem at all in going out after she came to the realization that the worst thing that could happen to her was that she might stand at a party by herself with no one to talk to. "It's not the end of the world if I don't have anybody to chitchat with." She said she would often go to parties and receptions unaccompanied by friends because she had moved to a new city and simply had no new friends. But every chance she would get, from a company bulletin-board posting of an event to happy hour at the higher-end clubs to wine-tasting charity events, she would "go it alone." She said that quite often if she maintained a relaxed expression and receptive body language, being alone was actually a benefit. People would come up and chat with her out of curiosity or perhaps even a bizarre kind of sympathy. "I didn't care if they felt sorry for me or not, as long as I could get out there and meet people." On more than one occasion she found herself feeling isolated with no one to talk to, and not making friends with anyone she wanted to maintain contact with. In these instances she simply left; it was not the end of the world.

Although I don't want to deliver a contradictory message, it's wisest to see both sides of the coin. Despite the fact that a woman alone gets more attention, a woman by herself is open to certain dangers. A man will be more likely to approach you, but he may also look at you as easy prey, or assume that you're eager, or (heaven forbid) easy. You're a lot more likely to be insulted, stalked, or assaulted if you're alone. That private one-on-one conversation can turn ugly or insulting within a matter of seconds if there's nobody around to listen in.

A night out with the girlfriends can truly be fun. A simple evening can lead to a night full of memories and a lifetime of laughs. Boyfriends may come and go, but good girlfriends are with you for life. Don't miss out on sisterhood and bonding because you're too worried about men. It's often when women are relaxed and happy and at peace with themselves that they catch some guy's eye and meet the love of their life.

David, a schoolteacher and trophy man from New York, says that he rarely approaches a woman who is with a group of her friends. It's just too intimidating. If he's with what he refers to as his "wingman" or a buddy watching his back and giving moral support, then he *may* approach a woman who is with her girlfriends. Otherwise, the stress associated with walking up to a big pack of women, and possibly facing rejection, is just too great. He explains, however, that a guy can usually tell if a woman is interested. She will make eye contact or spy him from across the room. If she's slick, she will find some way to momentarily detach herself from her group so that he can approach her alone, perhaps by making trips to the bar for a refill or to the bathroom.

I have heard a few notorious stories of women sending men a drink at a nightclub or a happy hour. This is a tricky prospect. On one hand, from a very basic point of view, you're taking the risk of blowing ten dollars on some guy who could be an absolute jackass. So what's ten dollars? It isn't very much money, but it can seem like a colossal waste if the guy simply winks at you, chugs down the drink, and doesn't bother to look your way for the rest of the evening. Another problem with the complimentary drink is that he might get the wrong message. It's dicey because you're a woman making the initial approach, and throwing alcohol in the mix (although you can't throw much else in the mix at a club or happy hour), and he might just interpret receiving a drink from a woman as sending the wrong message. Doing something like this makes it unequivocally obvious that you are interested and you're ready to meet him. You have to be honest with yourself and decide if you're able to deal with rejection.

I remember an embarrassing story of a certain supermodel who sent a bottle of champagne to the table of one of the "sexiest men alive." The story goes that he promptly sent the bottle of champagne back unopened. Yikes! But despite horror stories such as this, there is a chance you might send a drink to a receptive nice guy who takes it for just what it is—a sign that you are interested and would like to get to know him. You can usually tell if this is the case within the first few minutes of your conversation. But if he puts his hand on you, or comes over with one eyebrow raised and a silly "she wants me" expression, you should run, not walk, away from the situation.

Many women swear that you never get anything unless you go after it. Let me give you an extreme yet relevant example of how "going after it" can backfire in your face. Arturo is 6′5″, a handsome man with a master's degree in business administration and a C.P.A. A trophy man by all accounts. One night he and several of his friends were having a few drinks at an upscale club. After having a few rounds, and starting to feel a little tired, Arturo looked around the club and didn't notice any particularly attractive or interesting-looking women, so he figured it was time to go home. Just as he threw on his jacket and stepped off the curb to hail a cab, a woman came hurrying out of the club behind him, almost like a humorous scene out of a Spike Lee movie. She then handed him her business card and hurried down the street, waving and smiling over her shoulder. Once inside the cab, he looked at the back of the business card. In impeccable handwriting, it read, "Hi, 'Denzel.' I just love the Rams [Arturo was wearing a Rams football jersey]. Please call me. You're sweet."

Arturo could not believe it. He couldn't understand why a woman he hadn't even noticed—much less spoken to—for an entire evening could say that he was "sweet." He explained, "I knew, in the back of my mind, that nobody there had caught my eye, so I had this nagging doubt that this woman was just somebody I wouldn't have given a second thought to. On the other hand, there was something kind of wild about how she just threw her card at me with the note and all." He was not sure what to make of a woman who was so forward.

Ultimately (and understandably) he was flattered. The fact that the woman came on to Arturo was appealing to him. So he called her and they met for a drink. And he didn't find her attractive at all; she wasn't his type (for one thing, he prefers curvy, feminine women and she was a marathon runner with a hard, boyish body). But, she made it very clear to him that she liked him, and although he isn't interested in a relationship with her, he continues to see her from time to time, and responds to her emails. Why, you may wonder? Because he's a man, and while he's waiting for a woman he'd like to pursue, he needs something to occupy his time. You girls know what I mean. He realized that he can get something out of her, that it's freely available and being handed to him, so he does.

Obviously, this story illustrates the exception and not the rule. Most women would not run down the street handing out their business cards to guys they thought were cute, but the point still remains the same. A woman takes a great chance of being considered too pushy if she acts like she is interested in a man before he shows interest in her. Arturo put it quite bluntly, "I guess she wanted something." The fact that he said this with a sly smile made it clear exactly what he meant.

Many, if not most, women today are very careful about giving their home phone number to a man whom they've just met. This is exactly why so many people have Caller ID and unlisted phone numbers. Women have become so concerned about safety that quite often they have messages on their answering machines that are recorded in either a brother's or father's voice, or even that peculiar little computerized voice that is universally unidentifiable. Many women are careful to give their business phone number to a man when they first meet him. Giving someone your home phone number is a very intimate thing and, to a certain degree, means you are letting down your guard. Should the guy turn out to be a dud, or some type of sociopath, you have to go through the rigmarole of getting your phone number changed and the fear of having him find out exactly where you live or more about you than you are willing to divulge.

If you give a work number, try not to give your direct number at your desk. Give him either a switchboard number where an operator can then connect his call, or some type of voice-mail setup where you can retrieve his message and call him back. At least early in the relationship, this is perfectly acceptable. In an odd twist, when a man gives you his number, more often than not it is his home number. It is always wise to ask him for his work number as well, to make sure he does have a job. There are too many examples of women who have been given home numbers by a fellow because he has no other number to give. Of course, this is okay if he has an office in his house but, quite often, that is not the case. Women should expect to receive both a man's home phone number (because that is what he will give you) as well as his office number. If he is in some highly sensitive job where he is not allowed to receive calls, then deal with it. But if he seems uncomfortable or sneaky when you ask about his workplace, delve further into it to find out exactly why.

Telephone Etiquette When First Meeting a Trophy Man

- Keep your cool when meeting a man for the first time.

- **Do** take his phone number—his home phone number if offered, but preferably his work number.

- **Do** wait until a convenient time to call him. In fact, ask when it is best for him—nothing looks worse than being a worrywart and calling him during business meetings, when he is in the middle of some important project or presentation, or when he is in deep concentration.

- **Do** be firm in telling him that you would rather give your work number. Likewise, make sure you give him some type of time frame for when it is best for him to call you so that he doesn't bother you, the secretaries, or the switchboard operators, or clog the voice-mail system trying to get in touch with you at inopportune times.

- **Do** invest in Caller ID for your own safety.

- **Do** get an unlisted number. This is worth its weight in gold for ensuring a single woman's safety. (As one sister put it, "If someone does not know me well enough to know my phone number, they have no business calling me.")

- **Don't** give a man you have just met your home phone number. This can only mean trouble should things not work out the way you'd hoped.

- **Don't** assume that just because a guy has on a suit or seems well spoken that he is legitimate. Psychopaths and nut cases can sometimes put just as much or more effort into looking and talking the same way as someone who is truly worth getting to know.

- **Don't** ask a man for his number if he has not asked you for yours.

- **Don't** insult a man by lying if you don't want to give him your phone number. (We've heard the insulting lines from women who claim they are gay or married or involved with someone when they are really not, instead of just leveling with the guy and saying, "I'm not really interested, but thank you.")

- **Don't** give out any girlfriends' phone numbers to guys if you have not asked the sisters for permission.

- **Don't** set up a private meeting after the first tele-phone call. Start out in a safe, neutral, and cautious manner. Some wise women have even pre-purchased tickets to a movie, for example, saying, "I have two tickets a friend could not use. Would you like to go to the movies?" Orchestrate some type of public, fun meeting where you are safe and surrounded by others.

One word of caution. If you're going to be with a group of women, try not to go out with girlfriends who will absolutely outshine you in every way. You'll be stuck playing second fiddle. But if you have nothing but movie-star gorgeous friends, don't despair. Women automatically assume that a man wants the most beautiful woman. Not so. If a brother judges a woman *solely* by her looks, and you're always hanging out with your prettier friend, then you have a problem (assuming you're interested in him). But believe it or not, many men feel much more comfortable with what they perceive as an approachable woman. Some men assume that the gorgeous woman will reject him, and therefore focus on an attractive woman who is within reach. The girl next door often steals the show.

To avoid sinking your ship in the dating scene, it's wiser to go out with a woman who is a different type, or who has a completely different look than yours. If you're a corporate type, you might take your Afrocentric and artistic friend out on the town with you. If you're 5'2", full-figured, and a chatterbox, it may be better to hang out with your soft-spoken, rail-thin sister who is 5'10".

You can also go out with a married girlfriend or a couple. The idea of going out with another couple has many appealing factors. First, just like the old saying "misery loves company," happiness loves company, too. What I mean is that a young, loving couple with whom you share interests, who is not only happy together but going out and enjoying each other's company, is a good role model for both you and your date. You can't help but notice happy couples together, holding hands, especially if they're successful or have that certain image we all admire. Going out with an established couple or married friends also provides a certain amount of safety. Let's be serious; grown people don't need a chaperone. However, it is a lot harder for a woman to be date-raped if she is with friends who are looking out for her and insuring that she not only has a good time but remains safe and taken care of.

Going out on a date alone is very much like going on an interview. You could either feel very stressed and in the hot seat in a one-on-one situation, or more relaxed and at ease, with coworkers around to help you blend in. If it is difficult to break the ice, or if conversation is sluggish, having other friends around helps thaw things out. When you and your date reach an awkward point in the conversation, friends or married couples can jump in and pick up the ball, so to speak. Also, people seem to be more comfortable speaking within a group than one on one. Just take notice the next time you hear a guy talking casually about something like current events or pop culture. If he's alone with you, he may be more careful to measure his words, not wanting to offend you or, perhaps, even say what he *thinks* you want him to say. On the other hand, in a larger group where everyone has a little something to add into the mix, people are more prone to throw out their honest and independent attitudes and ideas because it seems like a safer zone.

My girlfriend Nia tells me she teases some of her girlfriends when they go out by threatening to approach a man they find attractive and say, "Hi, I'm Nia. I'm actually married but my girlfriend is not. May I introduce you to her?" Although Nia has never done this because she does not want to embarrass or mortify her single girlfriends, it really isn't such a terrible idea. A cute and light-hearted introduction such as this that actually leads a man to notice a nice woman, a woman with something on the ball who's actually a good prospect, might be appreciated. The tricky part is hoping the man of interest is actually a nice guy, too.

If you're going solo to a party or club, rely on your gut instincts and female intuition. Don't take stupid chances. The minute you feel uncomfortable with a man, get out of the situation. I can't help but remember a typical scenario told to me by a single male friend whom I consider a trophy man. We were talking during the holidays, and he was asking my advice about a girlfriend. He complained bitterly that the woman, who happened to be a very active and athletic woman in her late thirties, had gotten in a huff because he had touched her. I asked him exactly what he meant and he went on to explain how she had a great body, she was used to being admired, and she showed up for the date in a short skirt. He complained, "She knew she looked good and she wanted the attention, otherwise she wouldn't have worn something like that. I'm a very emotional kind of guy. I might have accidentally let my hand brush her knee, but it was no reason for her to get bent out of shape and tell me not to touch her."

I could see his side of the argument, but I could also understand exactly where the woman was coming from. On the one hand, our appearance can send a certain message. If a woman dresses like Foxy Brown, with hot pants, leather go-go boots, fishnet stockings, the works, she sends a certain image. It's unfair to even take the chance of enticing a man, then wonder why something uncomfortable happened. He put his hands on her (although he says it was innocent, I am *sure* it was not) because he thought she wanted him to. Yet, on the other hand, most women will agree that a man shouldn't get away with *anything* that makes you feel uncomfortable.

Love on the Job

Many men and women are hesitant to begin relationships at the workplace, partly because sexual harassment is such a sensitive issue. However, among the women who've married well, meeting men on the job was not only acceptable, it was considered preferable. For many women, the opportunity never came to meet the right man at school. Or perhaps a woman did have a serious romance in college, but the trophy man wouldn't commit to marriage. Whatever the case, women who weren't successful in school could network through work and career to meet trophy men.

It is perfectly natural to have some apprehensions about meeting men at work. But following a few guidelines helped these women avoid trouble. First, they dated only those men with more prestige or seniority than they had. Carla, a tobacco company executive, said, "Dating a subordinate is begging for trouble—it leaves an open door for the man to use you for his own professional gain, and if the love affair sours, he could accuse you of sexually harassing or discriminating against him. It's a no-win situation. Never date down with men in the workplace. Only date up. That way, if things go well, it may benefit you. If they don't, be woman enough to deal with the repercussions."

If dating a man from work makes you uneasy, venture to meet men with similar careers at other companies. Attend career summits or job fairs. Even if you're settled and quite happy at your current job, attending job fairs allows you to meet men who may be looking for romance. Likewise, professional trade meetings, conferences, continuing-education classes, and recertification classes can be a gold mine for meeting trophy men.

Be judicious about which conventions and conferences you choose to attend. Most of these conferences are highly specialized for specific professionals. A wise trophy wife told me to make sure to talk about the "fish out of water" concept. Take heed not to jump head-first into a gathering where you truly don't belong. For example, don't crash the party at a law convention if you're not in the legal profession. If you truly don't belong at a convention or professional conclave, you will surely stand out like a sore thumb. You'd better believe that if *you* know you don't belong, *other people* will know that you don't belong.

Don't Stumble Out of the Gate
on the First Date

LET'S TAKE A MOMENT AND PLAY THE "WHAT IF" GAME. What if you've met your dream trophy man? What if things have gone along at a perfect pace, you've shared a few easygoing phone conversations and a few witty emails, and he seems to be interested? Finally, he asks you on the first date. You are over the moon with anticipation and hope. The last thing you want to do is drop the ball. But, unfortunately, many sisters do just that, sometimes out of sheer nervousness, or sheer anxiety, or sometimes out of sheer desperation to finally make a relationship work. Many times a woman will unknowingly sabotage the first date and set the stage for inevitable disaster simply by the way she behaves and the way she comes across. First impressions *do count,* and they count for a lot more than we expect.

While interviewing several women, an interesting picture of the first date fleshed out before my eyes: a lovely evening, valet-parked car, wonderful dinner and conversation, mutual compliments, and a totally sexy and classy good-night kiss. How can it be? These women were wise enough to approach the first date with the Three C's: *care, caution,* and *consideration.*

Care

As hard as it may seem to believe, many women just don't care how they're perceived on the first date. "He should like me for who I am," they think. They just don't try, or they give the impression that the poor guy will have to work a little harder to attract them. These women recklessly try to get men to spend as much money as they can, they monopolize the conversation, they bring up taboo subjects, and then wonder why they never call back for a second date.

On the other hand, women who eventually married trophy men always took care to do the right thing, especially on the first date. First dates were not considered a "proving ground" to see how much the man could spend on them. When I asked them to describe their first dates, most remembered having dinner at a moderately priced restaurant. These were typically the more popular chains, places like T.G.I. Friday's, Applebee's, Outback Steakhouse, or Red Lobster. As hard as it might be for some sisters to believe, even the most affluent and financially secure men don't necessarily want to blow a couple of hundred dollars on dinner just to prove he is worthy of a woman. The truth of the matter is, women should not expect a man to shell out serious dough on the first date any more than she would want to. Going to a moderately priced, open, airy restaurant is a good start. This is not to say you have to allow him to be cheap. Taking you someplace like a hamburger franchise or taco joint just doesn't fly. But on the other hand, moderately priced and "hip" franchises usually have a friendly, casual atmosphere; allow for talk and relaxed conversation; and leave the woman feeling like she has had a good time without feeling obligated because the man spent a small fortune on the first date.

Many women remembered going to the movies on the first date. The couple would have dinner or a snack before or after the movies, while others would stop for a drink or cocktail afterward. The point was, they would keep the movie simple and light, nothing too heavy, nothing too gory or too scary. Taking the time to stop for a dinner or drinks afterward gave the couple a chance to talk and get to know each other.

Many women remembered going to a party. They were quite often privately thrown, or sometimes the public fund-raisers mentioned earlier. The beauty of a party is it allowed for a *safe* environment on the first date, where the woman was surrounded by friends or acquaintances and didn't feel too much "on the spot." If things got uncomfortable or if the man didn't seem as interested as she thought, being in an open crowd, with other individuals, gave them both a gracious exit.

The women who remembered going to a concert, music festival, or fine- or performing-art show considered this a nice, classy touch for a first date. Keep your mind open to new options; choosing this type of date says a lot about the man and his interests and, additionally, might broaden your horizons if you've never been to such events. Things like concerts or performance-art programs provide a nice chance to spread your wings and fine-tune your "cultural talents." A man usually appreciates a woman taking time to get dressed nicely, put on makeup, have her hair done, or really make an effort to look like a trophy woman. Venues like these allow both parties to put their best face forward.

Many women recall that their first serious date with a trophy man took place at a professional or amateur sports event. Quite often the women who met their husbands on college campuses would go to a college football or basketball game. Other women who met their trophy men later in life attended a professional sports event. Again, there is an inherent beauty to a date like this because the stress of being alone together is removed. You are literally surrounded by *thousands* of other people in a jovial atmosphere; there's time to talk and get acquainted, and yet there's opportunity for a graceful exit if things just don't seem to click.

Wise Women Understand the Subtleties of Role-Playing on the First Date

Some of you may wince when you read this, but you cannot shoot the messenger because of the message. The women I interviewed were very wise in not being the ones to make the first call or propose the first date. Those who did suggest the first date said they did so in a subtle way so that the man could ultimately take the lead. One woman bought theater tickets, then happened to *casually mention* to the trophy man she had the tickets and wondered if he would like to go with her. Otherwise, most of the women said they preferred, in fact enjoyed, the trophy man making the first call or proposing the first date.

Similarly, none of the women interviewed paid for the first date. As one sister put it, "It is nice to let a man be a man." Some women, attempting to seem nice or like modern working women, demand to pick up the tab. This only confuses the trophy man and gives him a mixed message. If a woman demands to pay for a date, he wonders whether or not she is truly romantically interested, or if she somehow doubts his ability to pay for the tab. Many trophy men are downright insulted, although they might subtly hide it. He disapproves of a woman wanting to pick up the tab, especially on the first date. One husband told me that his advice to women would be "If some joker lets you pay the tab on the first date, then something is definitely wrong. You should make it your business never to set up a second date with this kind of guy."

There were some other first-date subtleties and role-playing. For example, most of the women clearly remembered that they did not drive, that the trophy man came and picked them up, and that they did not specifically arrange for reservations or directions. There was something appealing, charming even, about the man taking the initiative and making the arrangements. Resist the urge to doubt this kind of occurrence. Well-mannered men are alive and well, and they "do the right thing" all of the time! To give him a feeling of male pride, the women customarily allowed the trophy man to decide *where* and *what* the first date would be. Of course, they might have subtly made suggestions, but the beauty of their "slychology" was in letting the man think that he was in control of things. Pushy women who jump out of the starting block sometimes scare men. Once again, the catchword is *care;* these women took *care* to avoid anything that might emasculate the man or hurt his feelings. There is nothing necessarily chauvinistic about this; in fact, there is something quite romantic and old-fashioned about it, and there is nothing wrong with being romantic or old-fashioned.

Several women gave me funny anecdotes about girlfriends they knew who actually had the nerve to complain if they thought their dates were too cheap or too stingy. This is a terrible faux pas. Of course, if the guy is such an idiot that he takes you to McDonald's or the rib-tip joint for your first date, you can just make the choice not to see him again. But if he has made a sincere effort and has taken you someplace reasonable, you come off looking like a bitch if you measure his worth by the size of the dinner tab. Nothing can turn off a man quicker than leading him to believe that you are simply in it for the money. The women married to trophy men could not stress enough how important it is to not only give the impression of *caring*, but actually behaving as though you are a *caring woman*.

Caution

The second of the three C's practiced by women on the first date with their trophy men was *caution*. These women were very cautious in how they carried themselves, the messages they put across to their trophy men, and laying the groundwork for the possibility of a future date if they, in fact, liked them.

They were cautious not to give the impression that they were trying to milk the guy. The average cost of the first date was generally somewhere between 30 and 50 dollars. This may not sound like a lot but, for a first date, it's quite reasonable. These women were always cautious, *always*, to have their first date at a public place or venue. They would no sooner invite a strange new man into their home, with nobody around to give them peace of mind, than they would play Russian roulette. Although they took pride in feeling like they had the ability to discern a trophy man from a dangerous man, they were cautious enough not to take any chances. Said one older woman, "Don't ever, ever let a man you just met into your home. It is one thing to allow someone you know inside the door to wait while you get your coat or purse, but not some man you just met. If you don't know him, you *really* don't know him." Whew! Cautious women are wise women. They took care not to have a prolonged visit at his or her home, before or after the date, implying that there might be sex. It can sabotage the chances of a serious relationship, and expose a woman to other, more serious dangers as well.

Similarly, they were quite cautious with the sexual image portrayed to their trophy men. "Good night" was kept short and sweet, perhaps accompanied by a peck on the cheek if they were interested, or a short kiss on the lips. The first date was no place for serious bumping and grinding. Many women could not stress strongly enough that the message you put out will affect the way you are perceived.

Consideration

The final of the three C's that women married to trophy men practiced during the first date was *consideration*. These women, perhaps, distinguished themselves from others by behaving in a considerate manner toward the trophy man. Imagine, for a moment, a short film clip out of a tawdry B-rated movie. A man and woman are on their first date. She teeters across the restaurant floor in front of him, wearing stiletto heels and shiny, cheap makeup, and a dress far too short and far too tight. He is a nice guy, and is somewhat taken aback by her appearance, yet is so excited to be on the date, he dares not complain. The waiter brings the menu, and she scratches her scalp with a long red fingernail. One of the rhinestones gets stuck in her weave. After sucking her teeth, and looking around the room to size things up, she places her order. Much to his horror, she orders Surf & Turf on Parade. It is the most expensive thing on the menu. The guy starts to shuffle in his seat, clearly uncomfortable. This only feeds her fire, and she decides to throw in a couple of extra things: pre-dinner drinks, appetizers, hors d'oeuvres, dessert, and a glass of port afterward. She also hurries to ask whether or not there is a cigar tray. At the blink of an eye she has run up the dinner tab sevenfold over what he had expected. A sister like this wonders why she's never asked on a second date. If only she would take a moment to reflect, she may realize that she lacked simple consideration. It's astonishing how many women miss the point. Men can see straight through shallow behavior like this. You must appear considerate if you want to attract an eligible or desirable man. Nobody likes a selfish woman. Nobody likes a lout.

Likewise, you should exercise consideration when choosing the topics that you discuss. Some women are so eager for things to work that they become nervous and say too much. Trophy wives advise single women to leave conversation about ex-boyfriends, ex-husbands, ex-lovers back at home. Sharing tawdry, heartbreaking, or bitter anecdotes about old flames with a new date is rude, inconsiderate, and idiotic.

Let's look at another imaginary film clip. A woman is ecstatic because a guy she has been interested in for so long has finally asked her out. He is everything she had always hoped for and dreamed of. He's well groomed, has a nice job, is ready to settle down, and enjoys a nice reputation in the city. He's well known and highly thought of. He doesn't make a ton of money, but he's shrewd with what he makes and is generally considered very giving and considerate. You've seen him around town at volunteer drives, at high-end happy hours, and at a few corporate-sponsored events. You're so excited to be on a first date with this man that something happens, *and you lose your mind.* At the dinner table you begin to tell him how much he is unlike your prior boyfriend. You start to give all sorts of sordid details about how your ex borrowed money from you, hid an illegitimate child from you, ran up your gasoline credit card, and played around with your coworker behind your back. It seems as though your alter ego has left your body, and you can't make her sit down and shut up. Somewhere between salad and dinner, you tell your trophy-man dream date how your ex broke your heart. You tell him how you never thought you'd get over him, how you thought you would never trust men again. You tell him all the gory details, as if he is a priest at confession instead of a first date. Not only does this type of behavior lack consideration, it scares off perfectly reasonable men. Is it any wonder that many men quite often are horrified by women who reveal too many of their old secrets? There is something touching, sad almost, about women who have been so traumatized or emotionally challenged that they sabotage the possibility of having a good time on something as simple as a first date. Yet it happens all the time. If a woman can remember those three key elements: *care, caution,* and *consideration,* then she'll find herself much better equipped, relaxed, and receptive to the possibility of a good time, perhaps even the start of a loving relationship with her trophy man.

The following are more important rules to consider during the first date with a trophy man.

Before the Date

Do dress tastefully. Trophy men love a woman who works hard at looking feminine. *Feminine* does not necessarily mean tight skirts, stiletto heels, or plunging necklines. Whatever you do, don't embarrass him or call unnecessary attention to yourself. A tasteful, expensive-looking, and classic outfit is a perfect choice. You can speak volumes with clothes like a creamy silk or satin blouse, bare shoulders or a smooth back on a warm summer night, simple silver or gold jewelry, simple slacks, or a feminine skirt that fits well. It's also safe to keep makeup to a minimum and nail polish neutral. Soft natural fabrics, simple expensive shoes, and well-made neutral ensembles are worth their weight in gold for dating and "investment" dressing.

Stay away from anything that's too tight, too shiny, or too clunky. You might scare him away with too much makeup or heavy overdrawn eyeliner. Forget sweatpants or exercise clothes. Don't go too tight or too sexy or have too much skin showing unless you want him to put his hands on you. Forget about the grunge look or the early-'80s Madonna look. And of course, forget about hairy legs, hairy armpits, bulging bra straps, run-over shoes, the hard-core "gangsta" look, or the "harsh" look.

Do try your best to simply be nice. Right off the bat, show some appreciation to the guy for taking you out. Although you don't have to act like you're some type of welfare case, it's a great boost to a man's ego to know you do appreciate him making the time to take you out and show you a good time. Good manners and graciousness can never be overrated.

Don't be late. Lateness is neither cute nor funny—especially on the first date. Guys are not amused by this and quite often think it is downright rude. If a trophy man says he will pick you up at eight o'clock, be ready at eight o'clock. Making him wait an extra half hour while you finish your hair is inconsiderate.

By the same token, if your date is going to be more than ten minutes late, he should have the courtesy to phone you. If he doesn't, he may not be a true trophy man. If he has not bothered to call you, and he is more than forty-five minutes late for a date, consider the date canceled and simply leave. If you are waiting for him at your house, you might consider not answering the door or simply undressing and getting "unready." If he dares to show up forty-five minutes to an hour late, tell him that you just assumed the date was off and decided to call it a night. It is important to let a man—any man—see that you have your own life and you are not just sitting around waiting on him.

When your trophy man shows up at your front door, and you know him well enough to let him in, take only a few minutes—don't draw things out. Make sure your home is picked up and tidy. Invite him to sit down but make sure that nobody in your home is there to harass him or put him through the third degree. If it is winter and you are wearing a wrap, extend it to him and let him help you put it on. This lets him see that you are used to good manners. Likewise, let him open and close doors for you (this is not a grudge match to see who is most independent).

During the Date
SHOW YOUR HOME TRAINING

Do allow him to go through his role-playing if this is important to him. In other words, let him open doors, help you on with your jacket or coat, help you in and out of the car, and follow you to the table. Another old-fashioned rule of thumb is if you are walking down the street, allow him to walk on the side closest to the curb. This might seem dated or extremely old-fashioned, but men, especially trophy men, relish the chance to behave like a gentleman. Some women we interviewed said that men were downright disappointed and offended when they acted too independent.

If you go to a public function or party with your trophy man, try to be gracious when meeting his friends. For example, look them in the eye, smile, and have a quick but charming response, such as "pleased to meet you," when introduced. Try your best to remember the names of the people you meet. If your first date involves dining out, follow the hostess or headwaiter to your table. Allow the hostess or head waiter to pull out your chair, unless they neglect to do so. Then your trophy man should step up to the plate.

Do reinforce what good choices he has made, if you are having a good time. Trophy men are sticklers for detail and often worry that perhaps the food wasn't just right, the drinks were too strong, or the table was in a draft. If he seems worried that you are not pleased, when indeed you are, make sure he knows how happy you are with the date.

Once seated at the dinner table, it's good manners to place your napkin on your lap immediately. (According to some of the older etiquette books, if you are at a dinner party, you wait until the hostess places her napkin in her lap before following with yours.)

It's bad form for a woman to order her own food. Tell your date what you would like to order when he asks and let him give the order to the waiter. Further down the line, if there are specifics, such as what type of bread you would like, or choice of salad, feel free to answer the waiter directly.

No matter how much money you think your trophy man has, it is in extremely bad taste to order the most expensive thing on the menu. I once had an acquaintance whom we used to jokingly call "Ms. Surf & Turf" behind her back, because she made a habit of ordering the most expensive thing on the menu. It was quite childish, considering that her dates did not always have the money to pay for such extravagant meals. No matter how coy or clever she thought she was, it was no surprise that she usually was not asked on a second date after this type of behavior. Take note: It is also critical that you do not order the cheapest thing on the menu. Although you might be going out of your way to seem well mannered, don't play yourself too cheap on the first date. Follow his lead by simply asking him, "And what do you think you will be ordering tonight?"

Make yourself familiar with place settings and serving utensils that are used at nicer restaurants. This can easily be done by looking in a bridal registry department, a *House and Garden*–type magazine, or if you are in a pinch, simply try to take your hostess's cue. If this is not possible, use the "outside–in rule"; in other words, you use the eating utensil farthest from the plate first and work inward, using the utensils nearest to the plate last.

If you are served bread, do not butter the entire piece of bread or dinner roll and chow down on it in one bite. Instead, break small pieces from the bread, one at a time, individually buttering each piece as you eat it. This is a subtle clue that you have table manners and "home training," as the old timers say.

Don't drink if there is food in your mouth. Likewise, don't cut up food on your plate into tiny pieces before you eat. This is only acceptable if you are twelve months old or younger!

Do not touch your hair while you are at the dinner table. Likewise, don't redo lipstick or put on makeup. This is why a bathroom is called a "powder room."

IT'S ALL ABOUT THE CONVERSATION

Do remain relaxed throughout the evening. A relaxed setting makes it easier to have an honest, meaningful conversation and will put your trophy man at ease. Try your hardest to ease any of his feelings of apprehension or nervousness during the first date. Trophy men don't like being put on the spot; they often have to deal with this type of stress on the job. The worst thing you could do on a first date is to act hard-to-get, ultra-sophisticated, or difficult to please.

Don't make your trophy man feel like the FBI is interrogating him. Unfortunately, women are often so eager to get to know the man that they launch into a long list of questions, barely giving the poor guy time to collect himself and think about his answers. This can be a definite turn-off.

Try to establish whether or not you share any common interest with him. If you are on a blind date, mention how you met the mutual friend who set you up on the date, and what type of interests, activities, or past you've had with this individual. Be careful, though; don't talk too much about the friend, otherwise it might take over the conversation.

Let him know that you have a life of your own and that you are an interesting, multi-faceted person. Don't ever give the impression that you have a plain, dull, ho-hum life. Everybody has a job, everybody has friends, everybody has a family, everybody has been somewhere or done something or takes interest in some type of hobby. You'd be surprised at how many positive things you can say about yourself.

Don't monopolize the conversation by constantly talking about yourself. Make a conscious effort to use the word *you* more than you use the word *I*. Oftentimes, when a woman is nervous and on her first blind date, she inadvertently babbles on too much about herself. Sure, the trophy man is probably curious, but you can drop bits and pieces of information without sounding like you are on a beauty pageant stage, giving a dissertation on why you should be the winner. You don't want to bore the guy or seem like you are self-centered. If you show interest in him and give him a chance to talk a little about himself, you end up hearing more in the long run and getting a better idea of what kind of man he is. And as one trophy husband told me, "What man doesn't like to hear himself talk?"

Be positive, but try not to act too overly dramatic or fake. Some girls gush, clap their hands, and ooh and aah at everything a man says. Guys can detect fake enthusiasm just like they can detect a fake accent.

Don't bring up his old girlfriends. If you do, you run the serious risk of appearing nosy, and you will appear to assume that you and the trophy man are going to become an official item. This might be a turn-off.

Don't talk about your old boyfriends. Nothing is worse than bad-mouthing your old flames to a new trophy man on a first date. It makes you seem small-minded if you have only bad stories to share; you risk looking weak, and who's to say the trophy man isn't listening to you and thinking, "She just might be talking about me the same way a few months from now!"

Don't bring up embarrassing topics about your family or his family. Who wants to know whether or not your father was in AA? Or that you've gotten a good price on your antidepressants? Or that you haven't saved a dime of your money and you've been working at the same job for five years? The first date is meant to be pleasurable, not a psychotherapy session.

Don't beat a dead horse, especially if it's about something that really doesn't matter when all is said and done. I knew of an otherwise brilliant sister who argued until the veins popped out in her temples about Anita Hill and Clarence Thomas. If this is a man you're interested in, don't run roughshod over the conversation on the first date. Complaining or arguing early on might do nothing but give him a bad taste in his mouth and cut off any possibility of a second date and beyond.

Don't, under any circumstances, begin talking about subjects that are too serious or "too heavy" on the first date. Let's say you are going out with the man of your dreams; why in the world would you begin to tell him how you are planning on getting married, having 3.5 children, and moving to the suburbs within the next year? You could alienate the trophy man—in fact, scare him to death. Instead of enticing him, you run the risk of making him think you are simply on a mission to get *any man,* and not necessarily him.

Don't allow the date to spiral downward into an X-rated slut fest. When I asked for advice from women married to trophy men to give to single women on first dates, most of them mentioned that you *never* sleep with a man on the first date, never let him put his hands on you, and never let things get out of hand. We're not talking about simply putting his arm around your shoulders at the movies or touching your hand over the dinner table. What the wives meant was no footsie under the table, no bumping and grinding on the dance floor, no serious heavy petting. Introducing sex into a relationship too soon—especially, heaven forbid, on the first date, only confuses things and causes your date to proceed in the wrong direction. You deserve and should demand more than simple physical pleasures, and you must behave accordingly.

I personally do not believe that a woman should ever make a move to pick up the tab. A woman may think that she is being well mannered by offering to pay for a date, but if she is romantically interested in the guy, and he allows her to pay—she only ends up with hurt feelings and a bad impression of him. Additionally, she sends him the message that she is strictly interested in a platonic friendship. Guys are often insecure and if a woman offers to pay the bill, he might wonder, "Why doesn't she think I can afford to pay for a date?" or "This girl isn't interested in me because she's making it obvious she just wants to be friends." Some women differ with me on this, pointing out that being independent and able to pay her own way is a plus when starting a relationship. If you feel more comfortable making some type of offer to pay, then I would recommend keeping it to a minimum; for example, allow him to pick up the tab when it is delivered to the table but sweetly offer to leave the tip, if you must.

After the Date

Do let him give you a good-night kiss—provided you like him and would like to see him again. The kiss should be appropriate; nothing too salacious or juicy. Tongue kissing on the first date might give him the wrong impression, just as shaking hands might be a turn-off. Most of the women interviewed could remember either a simple peck on the cheek or a quick, friendly kiss on the lips—not lingering too long yet just long enough to leave some hint of intrigue.

Don't allow a man into your apartment or follow him to his apartment, for any prolonged period of time, on the first date. It's a sad truth that trophy men can have misguided intentions, leading to undesirable consequences. People lose sight of their better judgment when they are nervous. Add a drink or two on top of this, and it's a recipe for potential disaster. Having a man you've just met linger at your apartment is loony. Get to know him first in a safe environment and then, if things click, invite him over at another time. One older trophy wife explained, "It's better to head off problems by never giving them the opportunity to start."

Do make sure to tell him you had a nice time if, indeed, you did, and that you are interested in going out on another date with him. Being a "mystery girl" might end up backfiring on you and leaving you in the dark if you don't give him any positive signs. If you were set up by a friend, tell that friend that you had a good time. The chances are great that your positive feedback will be carried back to him.

Don't complain about any aspect of the date. Unless he has taken you to some hole-in-the-wall hamburger drive-in or rib joint, give your trophy man the benefit of the doubt. He probably planned the first date based on what he could afford, where he felt comfortable, and where he thought you would enjoy yourself. If you didn't, don't be a whiny diva about it. Nobody, man or woman, likes to feel unappreciated. If everything except the setting or the food or the show was acceptable, let it go. Don't complain to the person who set you up, either.

If your date invited you to a party, a dinner, or social function, make sure to jot a quick thank-you note to the host or hostess of the event. Try to do it within a week, and keep it simple. Simply jot down your gratitude for the invitation and tell them how much you enjoyed yourself. This is a subtle touch that means a lot. Chances are that the host or hostess will mention to the trophy man how well mannered you were in sending a follow-up thank-you note.

Things Acceptable to Talk About on a First Date

- Him
- Current affairs in the news
- Local sports events, or developments with local or favorite sports teams
- His work
- Your work
- Places where you or he have traveled to and enjoyed
- Interesting articles or books recently read
- Observations about other acquaintances or mutual friends (be careful not to gossip)
- Movies, plays, or concerts
- Recent developments in pop culture

Topics You Should Avoid Discussing on a First Date

- Your old boyfriends
- His old girlfriends
- Money
- Weight problems or personal health problems
- His weight or personal health problems
- Other dates, successful or disastrous
- Age—neither yours nor his
- How you picked out your wardrobe
- Negative gossip about mutual friends or acquaintances
- Politics
- Sex (this is especially true if you want this guy to respect you and take you seriously)
- Death or depressing events

It's Only One Evening

It's easy to break it off with a man after the first date. If you see signs that he won't meet your criteria, don't ignore them. Just don't see him again. It's a waste of time. Be courteous, because he did make an effort to show you a good time, but don't string him along.

Big things to watch out for: If the man asks you for money, or gets up from the table or acts shaky when the bill comes, do not mistake this for an honest oversight. A guy who will shaft you for the bill on a first date should be avoided like the plague.

Also, if during the course of the date, the trophy man happens to casually mention that he is separated or estranged or about to get a divorce, immediately pay attention to the sirens that should be going off in your head. *Run, don't walk, in the opposite direction!* If indeed he has potential and is legitimate, you can reconnect after he gets his business in order. Make sure that he is not a married man. Make sure that he is not "in transition" with a problem marriage. Make sure that you won't be (accidentally) involved in a fatal attraction–type situation.

He Wasn't Always a Trophy Man

HAVING A PRECONCEIVED IDEA OF THE KIND OF MAN YOU'D like to marry isn't an indication of an elitist attitude. We have preferences in the types of careers we pursue, the neighborhoods we choose to live in, and the kinds of clothes we wear. So why shouldn't we have certain preferences for a mate? Men have always referred to the kind of woman who's their type. Many men cringe when they hear women use the phrase "He's not my type," but the plain truth is that people have individual tastes and preferences. Women get into trouble when they compromise the wrong way, settling for the wrong man because he's the best she has seen lately.

If you want to be married, it's important for you to *be selective* when dating. Just because a man is nice to you doesn't mean he likes you, let alone loves you. And even if he follows basic precepts like paying for dates when he invites you out, or calling when he says he'll call, that doesn't mean you owe him anything. The women who married well never confused good manners, common sense, or civility with being in love. And they never let men get away with misusing them because they were starved for love. These women set limits and expectations, and they lived by them. They were brave enough not to settle for anything less than what they felt they deserved.

Just as these women expect kindness, courtesy, and civility from their men, they're also careful to display the same qualities. They expect the same, if not higher, levels of achievement and success from their men. They'd no more date a man without gainful employment or serious goals than a member of royalty would marry a beggar. They expect ambition and drive from their men to match their own.

Let's consider Kirsten, a midlevel manager for a large telecommunications company. She's attractive, was educated at one of the big ten colleges, and works hard to keep her curvaceous figure at a perfect size fourteen. She's pretty much average in every way: dark brown hair neatly permed, simple tailored clothes from the Gap and Ann Taylor, modest travel experience, and hobbies like cooking and tennis. Kirsten is married to a handsome lawyer, two years her junior, who's on the fast track to becoming a judge in their hometown. In other words, her husband's a serious trophy man.

Women look at Kirsten with envy and wonder how she got him. For starters, Kirsten was very focused about what kind of men she dated seriously. It may sound cold, but she only dated professional men; some she interned with, others were either on a career track at her company or in graduate school at one of the university campuses in her town. Essentially, Kirsten set a standard for her men. She knew the kind of men she liked, knew where to find them, and concentrated on making things work. She took a risk; she might not have gotten what she wanted. But she knew she wouldn't get what she didn't want.

While women who marry trophy men set high standards for the kind of men they wanted, they were at the same time realistic about those standards. They understood what sort of man was within their grasp. You can set your sights on a professional athlete or a highly paid entertainer, but your chances will be slim and the competition will be rough. *Be realistic.* An absolutely perfect man doesn't really exist, but if he did, *would he want you?* Superstars want other superstars. That might be a bitter pill to swallow, but you have to be able to face some truthful self-evaluation.

We've all heard women say, "I'm too choosy," or "The kind of man I want doesn't exist." They shoot down any possibility of love or marriage with this silly attitude. Let's take the example of Katy, a friend of one of our subjects. Katy is an education specialist with the Board of Education in a major city, thirty, single, and still looking. She has waist-length hair, a Barbie-doll figure, and deep dimples—she's a real looker. Drop-dead gorgeous. And she's very particular about what her men should look like. A friend of hers played matchmaker, and introduced Katy to her husband's friend on a blind date. He was a terrific guy—a pharmaceutical rep with a major drug company, he owned a lovely home, was well respected in his church and fraternity, and was looking for a nice woman. After they went out a few times, Katy promptly gave him the cold shoulder. She complained that he was just too short. She thought that the fact that he bit his fingernails was "creepy." Of course, he wasn't really short, he just wasn't six feet tall. But Katy wanted the picture-perfect man; someone who was flawless. She was unwilling to consider a man who had so much to offer, and her unwillingness to compromise is why she is alone, and in all likelihood, will stay alone forever.

The women who marry trophy men understand the fine art of compromise. Yes, they're focused. Yes, they're real and committed to forming serious love relationships. And yes, they demand from themselves the same things they demand and expect from a husband. But, unlike many unmarried (or unmarriageable) women, they understand they might have to make concessions with their trophy men.

Mr. Right is not Mr. Perfect. Even trophy men have serious flaws and weaknesses that must be addressed. The well-married woman identifies these frailties in her trophy man early on, and makes short-term and long-term plans for compromise. She is willing to consider the right man, but not to settle for Mr. Wrong.

Recognizing a man's *potential* is key. After all, successful men had to start somewhere. Linda, who is marred to a computer executive, put it bluntly. "I knew my husband before he became a success. We go way back. But I saw something in him, I truly loved him, and I knew one day he'd be somebody. I hung in there when no other women looked twice at him."

Let's take another example of a well-married couple. You won't find any more of a power couple than Mya and her husband, Ted. They both are New Yorkers, and come from good families with strong backgrounds and home training. They both have dream jobs doing what they absolutely love, and they met each other and began their lifelong love affair while they were students at Harvard University. Mya pointed out to me that at many of the old, traditional Ivy League colleges, "there weren't so many of us." Because of a moderate age difference, Mya did not initially meet her husband until she was well into the middle of her education at Harvard. She remembers the day she met him as though it was yesterday. She was in the library and approached him with a question about a paper due in a class they both attended. They chatted for a while, she liked what she saw and vice versa, and then, being a gentleman, Ted escorted her from the library back to her dorm. There was something in the way he held the door open and gently brushed the small of her back with his hand that sent her over the moon. He was attentive, polished, and as soon as she saw the dimple in his cheek, she was a goner.

The next part of the story is something we can all relate to. She ran to her room to share with her friends the news that she had met this most incredible guy. But instead of her girlfriends oohing and aahing at the romantic treasure of Mya's meeting Ted, they simply replied, "We know him, that's the guy who dresses so dowdy." This was right around the time of the Ralph Lauren, Eddie Bauer yuppie look, and clothes, quite often, did make the man in the silly minds of a lot of undergrads.

But Mya was wise and saw through the foolish little issue of clothes. She remembered the smooth manners, and his fantastic academic plan for graduate school. She saw in him what the other women didn't see, and now she is happily married and firmly settled, while the "fashion seekers" who didn't like the way he dressed are still looking for a husband. Mya's not just married, she's very well married.

Similarly, let's consider Simone, a dermatologist married to a stockbroker. She remembers giving one of her best girlfriends the news she had become engaged to Anthony. But instead of congratulating Simone, her girlfriend replied, "But Anthony is so short!" As ludicrous as this might seem, replies and reactions such as these are so outrageous, there's no way they could be made up. The names have been changed to protect the innocent (and the guilty)! Needless to say, Simone is happily married with a couple of kids and, to this day, her husband's height is a non-issue.

This is not to say a woman should force herself to like or accept something she simply does not. If you have certain preferences, the old "apple and oranges" example—you should not settle for anything else. But, on the other hand, if certain minor attributes really don't make that much difference in the bigger picture, you should try to compromise or perhaps accept them instead of ruling out a potentially meaningful relationship because of stuff that just does not matter.

Although education is extremely important, *it is not mandatory that one be educated to succeed.* In many cases, the women who married trophy men were open-minded to successful men of all kinds. They respected men who were driven, with fast-track careers as entrepreneurs, realizing that many educated men fell back on their degrees and never did much with them. Said one woman, "There's nothing worse than an educated fool." Whether successful with a degree or without one, these women tried to judge men on their achievements. Ambition and drive count for much more in a man than easy money. As one woman so simply put it, "Money doesn't make the man...the man makes the money."

Sometimes trophy men are diamonds in the rough. A man's professional prominence might supersede his social graces. Trophy women understand that a man's rise to success could be rapid, not allowing him the time or exposure to learn the behaviors that come with old money. These women were willing to gently remind their men about social graces, help him with a thank-you letter, remind him which dinner glass was his, and expose him to people or experiences he might not have otherwise been exposed to. They even found themselves teaching their man the proper way to tie his tie. They gave self-confidence to shy men.

Don't misunderstand the message. I'm not advocating that you tolerate something you really don't like, or put up with anything you find repulsive. It's important to note that none of these women would have considered marrying a man with less education and earning potential than she. He had to have either one or the other. These women didn't tolerate men who were "finding themselves," and they never, ever provided financial support to boyfriends. But women who married well knew that physical flaws could be modified. Extra pounds can be shed, crooked teeth can get straightened with braces, and a thinning hairline can be shaved or ignored.

But here's a warning: Don't fall into the trap of trying to make a man into something he's not. If a woman refuses to accept limitations in a man and pushes him beyond his abilities, he'll fail in her eyes and so will the relationship. But you need to understand the worth of substance above style. Things like education, pedigree, compatibility, and earning potential are much more important than physical or sexual attributes. Who cares if a man has a thick neck when he treats you like a queen, is a good friend, and has the potential to become a successful husband and father?

Try to recall every guy you and your girlfriends have known who, at first, didn't seem like much, but then grew to become a good catch. We all know the old story of the one that got away. If we wrote these examples down as short stories and pieced the scraps of paper together in one long sheet, it would stretch from here to the moon and back again. It underscores the point of how Mr. Right can be just in front of your nose but, unless you have your goals, priorities, act, and desires together, he can slip right through your fingers.

The story of the ugly duckling that turned into a swan does not necessarily have to refer to a woman. It can happen to men as well. I can personally remember an "ugly duckling" from way back when—a guy who wasn't an outcast, but wasn't the most popular guy in high school either. He was too tall and too thin, with big feet. He wore thick glasses and his Afro never quite looked right. He was a bookish kind of guy, and never made the cut for the sports teams at his high school. People didn't dislike him, but he was simply unmemorable. He never would have ranked in a popularity contest.

Eventually, the ugly duckling grew up. He filled out, gaining a little weight in all the right places. He exchanged the thick glasses for contact lenses. Underneath that lopsided Afro was hidden a head of black, wavy curls. The man is certifiably fine, in fact. Of course, all that pales next to the fact that he went on to architectural school and now runs his own firm on the West Coast.

Because he has always been such a nice guy, he can't see

through the shallow sisters who now trip over their own designer pumps trying to get to him to just say hello; chomping at the bit to give him a chance now when they wouldn't have given him the time of day years back. As you can imagine, a few women are probably muttering, "I only wish I knew *then* what I know *now*."

The remarkable thing about stories like these is that not only can we all share a similar example, but despite the ultimate message, a lot of women still just don't get it. These detractors, who never gave the plain "fringe" men the time of day, kick themselves because the guy turned out to be nice-looking after all, or he is driving a great car, or he has a fantastic job. He's the guy who has his own fantastic business, or is a highly regarded member of the police force, the beloved fireman, on the fast track to becoming an army officer, or the teacher of the year in the biggest and most difficult inner-city high school. The silly sisters still don't realize that trivial things all fall away and what you're left with, at the end of it all, is the same person who has always been there.

When having conversations with the women who were married to trophy men, I was struck by the repetition of several key characteristics that these women admired. Most of them respected and desired intelligence in their mate. Likewise, most of them gained a great deal of self-worth from knowing that their man admired them for their intelligence and their achievements, and truly loved them.

Look Like a Wife if You Want to Attract a Husband

ALTHOUGH WOMEN OFTEN MAKE ALLOWANCES FOR A MAN'S style or appearance because she can see his ultimate potential, trophy men can afford to be much more selective. Unfortunately, the old double standard is alive and well. Men very rarely settle for women they don't find physically attractive. It seems shallow, and I know you've seen downright ugly men who, because of their success and status, have hoards of women running after them, but there's hardly any point to getting worked up over something that isn't going to change. Success, like power and influence, is like an aphrodisiac.

Morgan, a dentist's wife, beautifully summed it up. "There's no sense in women acting indignant about men judging them by their looks. It's unfair, but it is reality. When he first meets you, he takes in as much as he can see of your face, your body, your hair, your hands, your feet, and the whole package. If he likes what he sees, he'll move forward. If not, his impression in those first few seconds will sink you. But perhaps it's better that way, instead of being led on."

Fortunately, not all men share the exact same tastes, and what seems beautiful to one may be quite the opposite to another. Remember, some people like apples and others prefer oranges. There's a man for every woman, and vice versa. If you're not his type (meaning what a man personally prefers in facial characteristics, body shape, hair type, or skin color) *then move on.* You can't win, and you certainly can't argue your way into changing his mind.

It's been said that aggressive women go after their men, and savvy women make the first move. The truth of the matter is that if a man isn't attracted to you, it doesn't matter what you say or do. It's a losing proposition. And the same argument goes for men who prefer interracial dating. When trophy women are rejected, they take solace in knowing there is a man out there, a trophy man, who does consider them his type. If they suspect a man isn't attracted to them, they cut their losses and move on. One woman explained, "There's no point in yelling, 'Who the hell does he think he is?' If you're not his type, *you're not his type.* He doesn't have to look for other reasons to like you, or learn to like you, any more than you have to accept something you don't like." The smart woman knows when and how to let go. Many used the same basic principle themselves, understanding that preferences can be a very particular thing. After all, they weren't going to force themselves to accept men they weren't completely attracted to.

Instead, the women recognized their best assets and took extra measures to keep themselves attractive. Loving yourself, and feeling good about yourself can be a healthy driving force in your life, and feeling good about yourself involves keeping yourself looking good. Sherry has been married for several years to a talented and handsome television news anchor. She married him when both were in college at a major midwestern university with a top-notch journalism school. She's attractive and well kept, as you'd expect from the wife of a high-profile public figure. When she met her trophy man, she's proud to say that she looked her best. She wasn't wealthy, but she worked hard at keeping herself together. She remembers, "He saw me walking across campus. It was snowing, and I had on a red swing coat and a red cashmere scarf. I couldn't afford many clothes at that time in my life, but I'd splurged on that coat because I thought it made me look good. I must have made an impression sashaying across the snow because I caught his eye. He ran over to meet me because he liked what he saw."

Of course, clothes don't make the woman, but the first impression counts. Had Sherry dropped the ball with a poor first impression, her trophy man might never have sought her out. But he did. He liked what he saw and the rest is history.

The women who married trophy men routinely used other classy women as role models (sometimes their mothers, sometimes *his* mother). They perfected a look, using sensible and understated clothes, shoes, and purses. They bought the best things they could afford, with an eye toward choosing clothes that last: investment pieces, good designer wool suits, cashmere sweater sets, silk scarves, and things they knew would command attention in a classic, polished, and clean way. They understood how to look expensive without spending a fortune.

Women who married well made subtle enhancements that complemented their own attributes. For example, most of them permed their hair or used color highlights to match their complexion, preferring straightened, smooth, simple haircuts—never trendy or faddish styles. The older women rarely wore ethnic braids, but a few of the younger women wore groomed and sophisticated braids and locks. A few used hair extensions to add length to or thicken their own hair, but shied away from waist-length "showgirl" weaves. They regularly manicured their hands and pedicured their feet in basic reds or subtle, neutral colors like pink, beige, and peach. They avoided the thick, dragon-lady nails made of acrylic, considering them cheap and glitzy. Bright and shiny red anything—nails, lips, or cheeks—were reserved for black-tie celebrations and dramatic holiday events like Christmas parties.

All used makeup; usually lipstick, blush, and eye pencil or mascara. Most believed that heavy, dramatic makeup made them look dated and old. They favored name brands, believing that expensive makeup looked better on them and made a much nicer impression. Cara explained, "Men don't usually notice the little things. In fact, my husband wouldn't notice a change in my makeup. But, I've seen women pull cheap and broken cosmetic cases and lipstick tubes from their purses, and it looked so pitiful. I learned my lesson when I saw an old snapshot of myself, and my cheek blush looked greasy and streaked. Yuck! When I feel good about myself, and pamper myself with attention to the little things, I just look better."

These women tend to wear attractive underclothes and foundations. Even those with slender figures used well-made brassieres, panties, well-made underslips, and quality pantyhose. This attention to detail was not meant to be sexy or titillating, but instead made the women look well groomed. Even less expensive clothes look expensive if the proper undergarments make them hang correctly on a woman's body. All you have to do is look at the yearly best- and worst-dressed list of celebrities to see how some poor diva has made the worst-dressed list because she had on a poorly fitting bra and her chest was either hanging down or bursting out all over.

One gregarious woman told me, "I always used the rule of thumb that if I *wondered* if something didn't look right, it probably *didn't* look right. Nothing brings a lady down a notch quicker than jiggling boobs or a rumbling fanny." Her comment was funny, but it underscored an important point: Attention to detail set these women apart. Anything worn too tight or binding looks bad, even if a woman spends a fortune on it. Sure, revealing, tight, or suggestive clothes are attention-getting devices. Men may notice them, but *not* the way a woman looking for a committed relationship wants to be noticed.

What It Took to Get Him, It Takes to Keep Him

First impressions aren't the only situations where appearances matter. The women I spoke to practiced the old adage that "whatever it takes to get a man, it takes to keep him." They did not let themselves go. If he loved her hourglass figure, she kept it up. If she set the stage for romance with pretty lingerie and expensive perfume, she continued the practice well into the relationship. Her efforts were definitely noticed and appreciated: the smooth legs, hot tub baths, the perfume, and all things womanly. And they continued even when it seemed like too much of an an effort, or as though maybe he wasn't noticing. That made the difference, even when nothing was said.

Of course, this doesn't mean that a fifty-year-old woman should walk around with the same long hairstyle for thirty years just because she looked good with long hair when she first met her man. Nothing should be followed to an extreme. But a man always fears that the woman he was attracted to when he first met her is going to change into an unattractive hag once they get married. They notice when a woman lets her appearance go downhill, becoming unkempt and messy. Men especially notice those extra pounds. Trophy men don't like fat women, and they don't have to like them. Your figure and your weight are things you can control. If you're interested in a trophy man, you'll need to be consistent about maintaining your appearance. *Whatever it takes to attain something is also needed to maintain it.*

Too Much of a Good Thing Is Too Much of a Good Thing

It's easy for a woman to try too hard, especially if she's in love. She'll catch a glimpse of what she thinks appeals to her man and go overboard. He says red is his favorite color, and she wears red every day for a month. He likes long hair, so she plunks down eight hundred dollars on a weave she couldn't afford. He thinks the casual look is sexy, so she wears jeans to church. You get the point: Overdoing anything looks awful. This is a mistake that the women who married well avoided. An overzealous approach to makeup or dress comes off all wrong, especially with trophy men. The girls on music videos—plunging necklines, thongs rammed up their butts, torpedo breasts, big hair, and sculpted nails—are best left on television. The women who married trophy men sensed that working with what they had was much better than fantasy.

These women repeatedly condemned fakery. Plastic surgery at a certain age—face-lifts when they begin to show the signs of serious wrinkling and tummy tucks if childbirth left them with a midline bulge—was acceptable. But overall, they didn't believe in fooling Mother Nature with padded girdles and falsies in their bras. Masking a flaw will ultimately be discovered by her trophy man. (Just imagine your man running his fingers through your weave and getting the surprise of his life.) Well-married women never tried to look like something they weren't in order to fool a man into liking them. The masquerade can never last. It's better to hit the gym or visit a professional to help with skin or hair to correct fixable problems, instead of trying to patch over them.

Trophy women avoided shiny, cheap, and overpriced clothes. Most disliked purses with designers' initials all over them. Such showy displays of wealth show a lack of financial judgment. Monica put it nicely: "I never understood the single woman who pranced around in Louis Vuitton, Prada, Gucci, and gold everything.

"They looked so snobbish, so incredibly *overpriced*. I always wondered if a man would be too intimidated or put off by that look. What man in his right mind wants to finance a shopaholic?" Too much flash sends the wrong message and even worse, the wrong message to the wrong kind of man.

There is a disturbing trend in popular culture. Unfortunately, a lot of sisters are adopting this trend, and it might be for the worst. You know what I'm talking about. Just turn on the television, look at our popular entertainers, and you'll see rough-looking little girls shaking and grinding on the screen with thongs up their behinds and G-strings slung over their hips. They wear purple pasties on their boobs, and tattoos that look far better on an old marine than a young lady. We have seen them accepting awards with pasties on their chests. We have seen them with their hair bleached out, their nails glued on, diamonds affixed to their teeth and their eyeglasses, everything that is outrageous, over the top, and in bad taste. Of course, I am not suggesting that women should stifle their individuality, and I am certainly not suggesting that only clothes make a woman. It is one thing to be a "hoochy mama" on the television screen or video, and yet another thing to dress like that in reality. Ladies, please let's be honest and tasteful with ourselves.

On a humorous note, Mae West once said, "I want my clothes loose enough to prove I'm a lady . . . but tight enough to show 'em I'm a woman." Let's remember, you can dress sexy and attractive and still have taste. A man may like to have a little fun with a woman in go-go boots and a rubber dress, but he sure wouldn't want to take her home to meet his mom or raise his children.

There is a famous line from *An American in Paris,* where Gene Kelly's character looks at a woman and says, "That's quite a dress you almost have on." There is something a bit disappointing about seeing an attractive woman who otherwise looks fantastic, but has made the mistake of showing too much. It is in better taste to leave something to the imagination. If a woman wants a man to take her seriously, she has to play the part. It's no wonder some girls will dress like a floozy and then end up getting their feelings hurt when the guy wants nothing more from her than sex. Pay attention to the feminine details without being an overt exhibitionist. It is better to be *sexy* than to be *sexual,* as far as dressing is concerned.

A well-married woman understands she's an asset to her trophy man. He's proud to be seen with her on his arm, or to take her to company functions or on official business. They'd not dare embarrass their husbands with loud, brassy appearances, instead developing a style that works for them and sticking with it.

Think of these women: Maria Cole (Nat King Cole's wife), Camille Cosby (Bill Cosby's wife), Tracey Edmonds (Kenneth "Babyface" Edmonds's wife), Paulette Washington (Denzel Washington's wife), Grace Kelly, and Jackie Kennedy Onassis. They're all completely different, yet they all had something in common: They had the image, and they got their trophy men.

Before I go any further, I don't want to lead you to believe that the women we interviewed were drop-dead gorgeous or movie-star types. Quite the contrary. They were above average looking, but not raving beauties; intelligent but not necessarily brilliant; and more often average than out of the ordinary. However, something about them was quite extraordinary. They were the kind of women who looked well pulled together, and who took well-deserved personal time. They were the kind of women you notice when they walk into the room because you think to yourself just how much you would someday like to look the same. It is quite an accomplishment to be able to seem beautiful without necessarily being beautiful. It takes a lot of work to look great, to be memorable, and, at the same time, not seem like you are trying too hard.

None of them had the body of a ballet dancer or runway model, none of them were filthy rich, and none of them had designer clothes and top-of-the-line accessories. The great majority of them came from sound, middle-class families—comfortable, but by no means wealthy. Many of them seemed like your basic all-American women who were raised by loving parents and in strong households. They enjoyed travel and had traveled abroad; and a few could read and speak more than one language. The point to remember in all of this is that these women did not enjoy superstar status before they married their trophy men.

Although it might sound hokey, these women realize that it's what's inside that really counts. They felt that way about themselves and about the men whom they married. The common thread that bound these women was their ability to carry themselves with elegance and pride, impress and bond with his family and social circle, build a life and family with their trophy men based on similar values and hopes and dreams, and discern what qualities were important in their own lives and in the men they chose to live life with.

These women look rested, healthy, and happy. Of course, that is not to say they go about life being footloose and fancy free, like a Pollyanna. But something about them seems to say, "I have my act together." The fact that they were able to sit down and level with me about important and often personal details, yet were not intimidated or offended or paranoid, says something in and of itself. Some of you may automatically think, "How hard is it to seem settled if you, in fact, already have your life together and have a wonderful man?" Perhaps the most telling thing is that having the trophy man did not make the woman happy. She was happy, attractive, and appealing *well before* she met the man.

There is a quote that illustrates the points made here. The

quote has not so much to do with clothes as with image or appearance. Ann Richards, herself a larger-than-life figure, once said, "Appearance is a powerful thing. I know sometimes people can't remember a word you've said, but can tell you exactly what you were wearing." Ann Richards is a former governor of Texas. The point she makes is universal. People do judge you by appearance. How you feel about your life and your station in life is reflected in the image you portray.

As possibly goofy as it sounds, trophy women are often easily identifiable. They have on the lined slacks, the neat little sweater sets, the sensible shoes made from expensive leather. You can tell them a mile away, yet they were not video girls from MTV or poster-girl pinups. They were everyday women, just like you and me, who tried their hardest at looking their best.

SECRET #8:

Act Like a Wife if You Want to Attract a Husband

ONE'S IMAGE IS ALSO CLOSELY CONNECTED TO ONE'S BEHAVIOR. People are willing to teach social skills and morals to their children, but they're not always as willing to teach or groom their spouses. This is especially true of men, who may lack the time or patience to teach their wives what they feel they should already know. Trophy men are acutely aware of which women are groomed or socially "finished." They avoid rough edges in women like the plague.

Evin, a well-married woman, has a dear friend, Savannah, whom she's known all of her life. Savannah is almost like a sister, and just as one accepts the flaws of family members, Evin loves Savannah and overlooks her flaws. A single woman, Savannah is the life of the party. She always knows the dirty jokes and the sexy dances, and she can drink any man under the table. Evin often wished she could act as wild and carefree as Savannah. But, as they matured, the party-girl image and heavy drinking began to get old. Sixteen-year-old behavior doesn't look good on a grown woman, and it's begun to show on Savannah. So have the hard drinking and the constant cigarettes (or even worse, stinking cigars) hanging out of her mouth.

There's nothing appealing about passing out drunk, and having to be carried home by a designated driver, or acting sloppy because you're so sloshed. It looks downright pitiful on women. Evin never forgot the time that a male friend made a passing comment at a party about Savannah's behavior. "I'm glad my girlfriend doesn't act like Savannah," he said with pity and disgust. Loose behavior impresses losers, and turns off exactly the kind of men it's often meant to impress.

Trophy men want well-mannered, feminine, and dignified ladies. Women who married trophy men knew that letting a man see her embarrassing faults diminishes his view of her. After all, she might end up being his *wife,* and possibly even the *mother of his children.* Being seen drunk, cursing, sloppy, or high in public is out of the question. Most of the women we interviewed never ordered any alcoholic drinks stronger than a glass of white wine in front of their man, and never smoked in public in front of him, or in mixed company. They value their dignity, and realize trophy men value it, too. These women were extremely careful not to embarrass their trophy men, especially not publicly. Why would a trophy man, to whom image is important, risk the shame of being with an embarrassment?

Watch Your Mouth

Well-married women speak a certain way—they have been groomed to sound effortlessly polite, refined, and elegant. They understand that the way they speak affects whether others will judge or accept them. They used good grammar not just to impress their trophy men, but also for their own self-esteem. Popular vernacular is full of clumsy, incorrect usage that butchers the English language and makes women sound low-class. Invest in a simple grammar book from a local library or bookstore and practice, practice, practice.

Phrases You Should Avoid

"I'm all . . ." "He's all . . ." "She's all . . ."

"I says . . ."

"Duh" or "As if"

"I'm like" "She's like" "It's like"

"You a lie" or "Not!"

"I know that's right" or "You got that right"

"Axed" instead of *asked*

"Where's it at?"

"You and me should" instead of *you and I*

"I need to lay down" instead of *lie down*

Manners Matter

Polished manners make a woman a lady. Trophy men want polished, refined women as their wives. He can get boisterous, outrageous behavior from his friends, and trashy, flamboyant behavior from women who are girlfriend, not wife, material. Some of these reminders may seem obvious or even hilarious, but since manners classes and charm schools have mostly fallen by the wayside, modern-day women have unfortunately missed out on many of the basic lessons on what makes a lady. Nothing can sink a trophy man's first impression of a woman faster than bad manners. Even during our interviews, when relaxed and laughing like girlfriends, these ladies were careful to say "please," "thank you," and "excuse me."

Bungled Manners

1. Chewing gum with your mouth open (It's actually best that you not chew gum at all.)

2. Smacking your lips while eating your food or chewing with your mouth open

3. Scratching your scalp or body in public

4. Picking or scratching pimples in public

5. Pulling your panties out of your bottom or adjusting your pantyhose in public

6. Applying or touching up makeup at the breakfast, lunch, or dinner table

7. Leaving greasy or red lipstick stains on your glass (always carry a tissue)

8. Putting your elbows on the table during meals

9. Not knowing how to properly hold a knife and fork (It's difficult to explain, so observe and consult any older woman who knows how. This one is important, and a dead giveaway of an uncultured woman)

10. Putting off shampooing your hair just one more day, thinking no one will notice

11. Arriving for your date or appointments late (It's not fashionable—it's bad manners.)

12. Ordering the most expensive (or cheapest) item on the menu

13. Talking with food in your mouth

14. Biting direct chunks from your dinner roll instead of picking off tiny bites, piece by piece

15. Burping or passing gas publicly

16. Sucking or cleaning your teeth in public

17. Wearing pantyhose that have been mended with fingernail polish

18. Keeping an unmade bed or sloppy house

19. Not bathing or showering when you should, or assuming perfume can take the place of a bath

20. Forgetting to write a thank-you note when you've been given a gift, no matter how close the friend

As hard as it may be to believe, all these examples were witnessed, in living color! Oh my!

Some women would argue that style and behavior are inherited, gifts a woman is either born with or not. This may be true to a certain extent, however there are some self-help books that I would readily recommend. Five such books are *How to Be* by Harriette Cole, *Basic Black* by Karen Grigsby Bates and Karen E. Hudson, *The Handbook of Etiquette* by Emily Post, *Making Faces* by Kevyn Aucoin, and finally, *What Should I Wear? Dressing for Occasions* by Kim Johnson-Gross and Jeff Stone. These books cover everything from etiquette, modern-day protocol, and rules for dressing, all the way to choice of fragrance and makeup application.

One final word. A sound bit of advice was given to me by a former research assistant. She pointed out that it is often helpful to identify and mimic the manners, good habits, and dress of a role model. It is easier to learn by copying someone you admire. "There was an older Ph.D. who worked at my company who always looked fantastic and was well respected. I would follow her cue on what to wear on dress-down Friday, what to wear to company functions, how to look appropriate and put the best picture forward. I noticed that she never had on any sloppy sweatpants or silly outfits on casual days, and it only took me one time to make that mistake. I also noticed, when her husband would pick her up to drive out of the city for the weekend, how she was dressed. At Christmas functions at the company and at formals sponsored for benefits in the city, I would look to her to see what type of dressy outfit she would wear. Come to think of it, I probably studied every detail about that woman. Although we looked nothing like each other, I tried to adopt her image and make it work for me. It was probably the smartest thing I ever did, because she never took a misstep and I imagine it took her years to perfect that perfect image."

Kiss a Few Frogs and
Forget Them

SO NOW YOU'VE GOTTEN YOUR LIFE IN ORDER, YOU'VE focused on developing yourself, and you've met a man. The two of you have struck up a wonderful camaraderie, and the relationship seems to be moving forward. He wants to meet your parents. He wants to be physically intimate. Here's where you need to pause and really look objectively at what is happening. Is this man really marriage material?

The turning point in a relationship, where a woman asks herself if her boyfriend is marriage material differs from one couple to the next. There is no "schedule," per se, because what is a watershed moment in a relationship for one woman might be very different for another. When is it serious? Could it be three months? Could it be six months? This is a gray area, because some women have no problem going on with a relationship for several years before they expect a true commitment from a man, or ask themselves if they personally want the relationship to go further. On the other hand, some women become irate if they feel like they're being strung along for longer than a couple of months. Only you yourself can identify your own comfort zone with your man.

Human nature is a funny thing. Women quite often have a nagging gut feeling that they ignore because the message is one they don't want to hear. Listen to what he says, watch how he acts, and, if a man does *not* seem like he's going to take you seriously or take steps to commit when you think he should, it's best to move on. No good comes from being strung along. Although it's difficult to quantify this type of thing, because sisters never really want to admit how long the trophy man has avoided commitment, *if you've been going out for many months, and been intimate with a man, then he should have the decency—and honor—to address your concerns about commitment.*

The women who married trophy men asked themselves the following three questions when they'd been dating a particular man seriously:

1. **What about this man and our relationship is truthful?**

2. **What about this man and our relationship is meaningful?**

3. **What about this man and our relationship is valuable?**

Now, I know some of you are cringing because love wasn't mentioned in these questions. But women who married well realize that love alone cannot be a woman's sole guide in evaluating her relationships. We all know couples who loved each other deeply, but were unable to make their relationship work or keep their marriage together. Quite often, the failure resulted because the couple hadn't taken the time to realistically answer those three questions.

Assessing what is truthful, meaningful, and valuable in your relationship is of utmost importance. Of course, you must love your mate, but it's a hard truth to accept that love alone does not help you feel good about yourself; develop you or your husband as individuals; help you pursue your dreams and goals, both together and independently; help make important decisions on having children, and raising them; or help to meet the responsibilities of paying for the house, tuition, insurance, and retirement. Life goes on and women (as well as men) do not live by love alone.

Head-over-heels love doesn't last. No matter who you are, and no matter how much you love your man, as time goes by the infatuation and lust fade and all you're left with is the two of you. But take heart, *because once the romance fades, the serious everyday business of love can begin.* If your relationship is anchored in what's real, truthful, and valuable, there will be no explosive breakup or bitter divorce when you realize that things aren't quite the way they used to be. The women who married well took a more pragmatic approach to "making the relationship last."

The men whom they eventually married were often considered best friends and confidants, not just a terrific roll in the hay. Comfortable, sustaining love is often built on hope and friendship. Friends make good spouses, and it requires patience to allow a love affair to blossom from a friendship.

In addition to friendship, women who marry trophy men have highly defined criteria for compatibility. They believe a man's family background can make him desirable, and pay close attention to the family values that have been seeded since childhood. They look for men with the same expectations and values regarding children and parenting.

Women will either consciously or subconsciously pick men with similar political ideologies. Likewise, they commonly marry men who have similar views on religion. In many instances, women and their mates shared some common interests in hobbies, sports, and pleasurable pastimes. I can think of several couples who enjoy tennis together, and several who took golf trips. A particularly interesting couple enjoyed diving when they first met and continued to do this even after they had their children.

Another example of a key compatibility area was financial earning power and educational background. It's most unusual for a woman to feel perfectly at ease about earning much more than her husband. It takes a strong man (indeed, an unusual man) to not have any reservations about his wife's being the breadwinner. Although this is acceptable and is certainly not unheard of, a woman has to take into consideration the male ego, and knowing that she cannot necessarily lean on him during hard times.

This is also the point at which the wise woman did a little bit of investigating into the man she was dating. It may sound callous, but you don't want to be misled or waste time with imposters (either dangerous or disappointing ones). *Men will lie if they have something to hide,* and if they think they can get away with it. One woman explained, "Whenever I met a man, I would casually learn as much as I could about him. It wasn't an interrogation or anything like that. And I generally sensed he did the same to me. The only men who were offended by my subtle questions were those who had something to hide. I checked out and verified everything I could about him."

Many other women did the same. They found excuses to meet his old classmates, studied his yearbooks and fraternity directories, looked for old school photos, and asked to see his diplomas and degrees. Many simply called the office of the registrar or alumni affairs to double-check suspicious stories about college or school. The same can be done with local directories of the Better Business Bureau, Chamber of Commerce, or small-business directories if he owns his own business.

They would routinely verify the man's job. They wouldn't

just call, but instead would personally check out his workplace, making the excuse of taking him to lunch or dropping off a gift or some trinket for a special occasion. If things were as he'd said, everybody benefited; if not, it was better to find out early than be hurt or disappointed later on. Chances are this should be pretty easy, because the average guy tries to get you to his house or apartment as soon as he can! If he doesn't, then a lightbulb should go off in your head automatically. Why does he seem to be hiding from you? Find out his address and his neighborhood, and then make sure to discreetly check them out. Take a girlfriend for safety. If it is in a rundown part of town, ask yourself why. Is he simply a young student starting out who can't afford better, or does this man lead a double lifestyle? If something about the picture doesn't fit, then surely there might be something wrong. Does he live in a dormitory although he is not a student? Does he have any roommates? If so, what type of characters are they? If they seem to be constantly drunk, high, or "freaky," then that should raise your suspicion.

How about this as an example: Does he live with his mother? Of course there may be nothing wrong with his mother, but if he is a grown man, finished with school, with a wage-earning job, why is he still under her wing? It's one thing if she is infirm and needs his help, but it is quite another if this is not the case. If he doesn't live with his mother, does he live next door or within arm's reach? This is very telling. You may have heard the nightmare story about the boyfriend who is pretending to live with his mother but is actually living with a girlfriend. This and other stunts have been pulled off by many a man.

Another "cat in the bag" is the married man. I remember hearing a story from a girlfriend years ago when she was in graduate school. She met a nice guy at a happy hour who seemed to be absolutely enthralled with her. He tried to play the role of a young broker just starting out, but she did a little snooping by tracking down his home address through his secretary, under the guise of being an old classmate from out of town who wanted to send a Christmas package. Sure enough, she found he lived in a suburban, bedroom community, in a large house complete with a swimming pool, cabana, and swing set for the kids in the back-yard. This would have been a charming picture except for the fact that she found out that this joker was married with kids.

It also pays to try to find out early in the relationship where a man spends his free time. Does he spend every waking hour at the gym, or does he hang out after work and on the weekends at neighborhood bars that you wouldn't be caught dead in? It shouldn't take a woman being burned too many times to find out that things are quite often not what they appear to be. Consider all those good-looking guys in business suits who seem like they have good sense, yet hang out at topless bars or dives where you thought only thugs went. This type of behavior, unfortunately, says a lot about a man.

Finally, it might seem cynical, but if a guy seems too good to be true, he might be too good to be true. What do I mean by this? If a guy, within the first week of meeting you, tells you that he volunteers at the Humane Society, that he goes over to the local nursery schools to read to children, that he spends certain days of the week pushing around handicapped seniors in their wheelchairs in a nursing home, that he visits his elderly parents and drops off a basket of money to them, and, finally, that he substitutes for his pastor every other week, then this might also mean that your new fella has a problem with the truth. Ha!

Trophy women also admitted to investigating their man's finances. Not in a tasteless, prying fashion, and certainly not by asking point blank what he earned. Men are turned off by auda-cious questions regarding their salary. But ballpark salaries can be determined by comparing friends with similar jobs. I am certainly not advocating that you subject your man to a rigorous set of third-degree questioning during your dating process. In fact, if you come on too strong, it can backfire and send him running in the opposite direction, thinking you are nothing more than a gold digger.

Questions You Can Ask to Gain Financial Information Without Seeming Too Snoopy

1. How is the job market these days for a[n] (analyst, engineer, high-school teacher, physician assistant)?

2. Do you find it difficult to deal with student loans? (This is a very subtle question; his answer might indicate that he started off with a financial foothold if he didn't have to have a student loan, and if he *did* have student loans, he might begin to jokingly complain about how easy or how difficult it is to make the payments.)

3. As a single man, what do you think about renting versus owning?

4. How competitive is the job market in this area (the South, Midwest, far West, Eastern seaboard) for your type of job?

5. How did you consider your income when you were making career decisions? (This question is very basic and fair, yet telling. You'll learn from his answer whether or not money was a major factor and whether or not he brags about the amount of money he's making.)

6. My cousin is also a (writer, radiologist, systems analyst, pharmaceutical representative). Do you think he could do a lot better out here than in Nebraska?

7. Does the cost of living bother you here? (This is a particularly good question for those who live on the East Coast or West Coast. If he matter-of-factly says that paying the average exorbitant rent in a city like New York, L.A., San Francisco, or Honolulu doesn't bother him, you can assume he is probably making pretty good money.)

8. If he is not in a commuting area where he takes the train, ask him about his car. (This is very telling, although many men, especially younger men, will spend a good deal of their liquid income on their car.)

These women also discreetly found out if he had good credit, if he was in debt, if he'd prepared for retirement, or if he had dependent parents, family, or children. They noted their man's spending habits. If he was incredibly cheap or foolishly extravagant, they wanted to know about it. If he'd had a repossessed car or a revoked credit card, they wanted to know about it. If she remained oblivious to his money problems, the very same problems could begin to involve her.

Lightning doesn't always strike the first time around. Rarely, if ever, did a woman automatically meet her trophy man (the love of her life), marry him, and then live happily ever after. That's a fairy tale that's been fed to us from Hollywood. Love at first sight is a fantasy. And those of us who believed that we'd experienced it, had actually only felt lust or infatuation at first sight. The women who married trophy men had to weed through countless men—through the pain of rejection, heartbreak, and anger—before they found the genuine article. Quite often, the pain and disappointment was inflicted by someone whom they were quite sure they'd fallen in love with at first sight. But ultimately, they were able to assess the problems and look at things realistically by working past their infatuation, and working toward real love.

If they realized that the relationship wasn't on the path to commitment, they cut their losses early and continued to look for their trophy man. If a boyfriend was just out for fun, they didn't languish. Instead they continued to look for something serious. And, more important, these women avoided bitterness after the breakups. Bitterness that isn't shaken off accumulates, only to surface at the wrong time with the right man.

Mending a broken heart is not easy. There is a classic commercial where a young woman comes into a gasoline station/convenience store and buys two dollars' worth of gas, two pints of Häagen-Dazs ice cream, and a box of tissues. When she lays her credit card on the counter, the girl behind the cash register gives her a sympathetic pat on the hand. She has obviously just broken up. Who among us cannot relate to the old "box of Kleenex and half gallon of ice cream" feeling when a heart is broken?

It's glib, unrealistic, as well as insensitive to give advice that says, "Just get over it." Hearts and emotions are frail things, and quite often it takes time to get over a relationship. One woman told us that after she broke up with her boyfriend of several years, she could barely get her life together. "I felt like I had hit a wall. Everything that I had worked and hoped and dreamed for came to a screeching halt. I felt completely depressed and, in fact, even thought about going to see somebody to take some type of medication. But slowly I was able to work it through. I talked with my sister, with whom I knew I could share anything. She made me feel better by admitting to me that she'd had her heart broken, too. You know the old adage—'misery loves company.' Also I think it really helped me to focus on something else. I planned a trip to the Grand Canyon with one of my girlfriends and ended up having the time of my life. When I got back, of course, I didn't have a new boyfriend and didn't fall in love on the trip— but it's an experience I will never forget." Other women have advised us that when they have a broken heart, they simply try to throw themselves into their work or hobbies so they don't fixate on the negative aspects of a lost relationship. The last thing you want to do is sit by the phone, waiting for it to ring. Sadly, a lot of women do wait, hope, and pray for a broken relationship to come back together, but quite often, the only thing that happens is the guy will come slinking back to use the woman because she is so emotionally frail. This was wise advice from an older woman: "If he made a fool of me once, shame on him; if he makes a fool of me twice, shame on me."

SECRET #10:

A Sample Is Ample

THE MESSAGES ABOUT SEX FROM THE WOMEN INTERVIEWED were complex. Perhaps they seemed so complex because the very act of sex itself means many different things to different people.

A generation ago, women were taught to believe that "good girls don't put out," and that men wanted innocent and pure virgins as their wives. Then came the sexual revolution, and women decided that they wanted to sow their wild oats and get a little experience, too. But somebody must have forgotten to tell men this, because even decades later they still hold on to the myth of "good girls" and "bad girls."

Lo and behold, modern problems like AIDS, venereal disease, and unwanted pregnancy have brought people's views full circle, and women have toned down their appetite for unabashed sex. Attitudes that would have simply been considered "liberal" or "laid back" a few years ago are now downright dangerous—even suicidal—in the new millennium. Wise women would no more sleep with a man they don't know than put a loaded gun to their head to play Russian roulette. It's dangerous to be too liberated, and many women realize that a smarter approach to sex leaves them less worried and more likely to land a husband.

Most of what I've learned during my talks with women regarding sex and the trophy man refutes modern-day assumptions. Some of their attitudes sound as if they were plucked from the forties and fifties—certainly not the behavior of women in the new millennium. But rest assured in the importance of the message. Getting women to open up and talk about sex is very difficult. So difficult that their messages cannot be ignored.

Most men, trophy men included, will gladly screw a woman if given the chance. Sex is often purely physical to men; a recreational activity that can be practiced for the sheer fun of it without emotional baggage, love, or even affection. Yet many believe "good girls" (the kind of girls they'd marry) don't sleep around. Of course, this double standard doesn't make sense—guys should realize if they all screw as many women as they can, not too many "pristine" women will be left to marry. But it's hard to argue with hypocrites. So the ladies I spoke with didn't argue, and surely didn't try to prove men wrong by portraying themselves as sexually liberated or experienced. Instead, it could be said that these women *played the game slicker.*

Sydney is a human-resources administrator married to a pharmacist. She chuckled when she told us, "My conservative husband did everything he could to try to get me into the sack when we first met. You name it: offering me drinks, telling me he was madly infatuated with me, and going so far as claiming we were physical soul mates. But I didn't give in. I made him wait. And later, he told me the anticipation and suspense made him want me more. I truly think he loved me more because I *didn't* give it up."

What these women realized was that men—trophy men included—have fragile egos. And a fragile male ego worries, "If she sleeps with me so easily, who else has she been with?" In the back of his mind, he will wonder if you are comparing his performance as a lover with that of the men you've slept with in the past. Similarly, men are absolutely suspicious of (and ultimately turned off by) women who seem to know too much in bed. After all, where did the sexually experienced women get all that practice?

If you come across a truly liberated trophy man who is not in any way intimidated by a sexually adroit woman (and these men can probably be counted on one hand), it's still not in your best interest to go to bed with him early in the relationship. A husband of one of the women interviewed felt free to explain. Men, especially *successful* men, are quite often able to get all the sex they want. Because they're considered a good catch, women (and particularly party girls, freaks, and fun-seekers) often chase them and offer themselves on a silver platter. A trophy man has all the sex he wants, so easy intercourse only momentarily excites or intrigues him. In fact, it's rather blasé. However, if you provide a challenge to him, you will distinguish yourself from all of the others.

Women are more likely to associate sex with love, and quite often have sex with a man hoping and believing it will lead to love. If she sleeps with a man, especially early in the relationship, in an attempt to make him love her, it might as well be romantic suicide. Men have an idealized view of the women they marry, and the image doesn't include "an easy lay."

Here's where many women's hackles will go up, because virginity in adulthood in this day and age is almost unheard of. Additionally, if a woman becomes seriously involved with a trophy man, the odds are pretty high she's going to sleep with him, right? Of course. The women who married trophy men had to become sexually shrewd. By *sexually shrewd,* I mean that well-married women carefully weighed their decisions of when and why they slept with their trophy men. Here are some of the unspoken but closely followed principles of the sexually shrewd woman.

- The sexually shrewd woman never, ever sleeps with a man on the first date. *Never.* She knows that she'll end up regretting it, especially if she likes the man. She understands that the trophy man will lose respect for her if she doesn't make him wait, and so holds out as long as possible. Many held out for as long as humanly possible, months to years. All of the women I spoke to limited expressions of affection (hand-holding and kissing) on their first date. None had intercourse or oral sex on the first date, or early in the relationship, for that matter. Many of the women interviewed waited months before having serious intimacy. (The fact that none would answer me directly when asked, "How long did you wait?" illustrates just how serious and discreet these sisters were). And the longer the wait, the better.

  Undoubtedly many of you are probably wondering, "How long to hold out? How long is long? Who decides how long is long?" Of course, these are delicate and very tempting questions. They're tempting because everyone wants to know if there are general rules of thumb that the more fortunate women follow. But it's difficult—no, it's impossible—to ask a woman directly, and have her answer in a straightforward manner, exactly when she first slept with her man. Some things are just too personal to discuss in public, and are so private that they really should be cherished. Suffice it to say that I got the general idea that the women married to trophy men knew it was important to wait as long as possible. When I would press them for specifics, I would get an answer, again and again, that corresponded with the notion that men consider women who sleep with them too soon to be too easy. Women considered it important that the man knew them well enough first. They didn't want him to start taking the relationship for granted and focus only on the sex because they had been intimate with him too soon. They wanted to feel they were in a solid and loving relationship before they had sex. If they thought the relationship showed promise of a future, they tended to try to hold out and conserve themselves and delay consummating the relationship. Of course, the perfect time in a relationship is when there is a certain amount of intimacy, mutual affection, love, and trust. This varies on an individual basis and only you can decide when.

I personally know of a woman who began a long-distance relationship with a patent attorney when she lived in Connecticut and he lived in Chicago. As crazy as she was about this man, she wanted him to take her seriously. The first time he flew east to visit her, she literally went out and bought a Jennifer Convertibles couch to make "damn sure" he didn't come to her condo and flop into her bed. She made her trophy man believe he was really dealing with someone special. Goofy? No! She fell into a relationship, instead of a bed, and now ten years later, she's married to him. "I didn't have the money to buy a couch, but it was the best thing I've ever purchased. He actually appreciated the pressure of the whole sex thing being off of him, and was sort of relieved he didn't have to perform. He left with an intact image of me being a special girl, and I didn't have to rack my brain wondering if he'd call, if I'd gone too far, or if he would turn out to simply be another hit-and-run kind of guy."

One important thing to remember, should you sleep with a man too early, is you don't want to sabotage your chances of intimacy and find yourself wondering, "Did I do it too soon?" It goes without saying that you don't have to deal with this question if you *don't force yourself* to. The decision to become physically intimate with your man is more about a feeling of commitment than an actual timeline. It's of tantamount importance. Do you know if he's healthy and free of disease? What about HIV? You should know, if you value your life! Would you feel comforted by him if you accidentally became pregnant? A sexual relationship is no joke. It is foolish for a woman to say, "When we reach X number of months, then I will let him have some." She should, instead, gauge his behavior, her own behavior, their feeling of commitment and love, and their genuine level of maturity.

One wise sister pointed out an often overlooked fact regarding sex and intimacy. She didn't want to sound prudish, but it rang true. "In many ways, sex can be overrated. When we bring it into a relationship, it nudges out other equally important factors. It has a way of clouding issues and making us concentrate less on the things that really are important. A healthy physical and spiritual attitude about our bodies is important. But let's keep things in perspective. You marry and live your life with a man, not his crotch." It's almost as if you rob yourself of things that are really important if you hurry through the enjoyable stages of a developing relationship: initial attraction, longing and infatuation, the dating game, and finally the intimacy. When you skip from one point to the other, you miss a lot of beautiful things in between.

- The sexually shrewd woman does not fool herself into believing that she could mesmerize her man early on in a relationship by being erotic or freaky. It sets a bad precedent that will sabotage the chance for meaningful intimacy. It's particularly deadly to brag about an insatiable sexual appetite or superhuman endurance. It may titillate initially, but ultimately it does nothing but demote a woman to "screw status."

- Although most of the women I spoke to had at least one sexual relationship before meeting their trophy men (and often had three or more previous sexual partners), the sexually shrewd woman *never* discussed specific details about their previous lovers with their trophy men. Nor did they ask their trophy men for specific details about their sexual past.

The way a lady conducts herself sexually can make or break a relationship with a trophy man. Let's take the example of Deidre. She's thirty-five, works as a systems analyst for a large company, and was introduced to a trophy man through her cousin. They went to an expensive restaurant for their first date, checked out a jazz club afterward, and then went back to her apartment. She invited him in for drinks, and a terrific conversation turned into serious fooling around. Before she knew it, she was in bed with him. Right then and there, they made passionate love. Deidre told her girlfriend she was determined to show him she was "the best piece of ass he'd ever had."

Deidre had the little voice of warning in her head, but she reasoned that it was really okay to sleep with him. They were instantly attracted to each other, and neither one of them were virgins, anyway. She liked him, and wanted to give him a preview of what was yet to come. They were both adults well into their thirties. And if he liked her, great sex just added to his attraction, right?

Wrong. Deidre had it all wrong. Of course, the guy began hot and heavy, and then started slacking off after a couple of weeks, gradually letting things die a natural death. He'd initially liked her, but something about her willingness to sleep with him so early and so easily dampened his view of her. This trophy man wondered if he'd want to get serious with, let alone marry, the kind of women who'd have sex with him on the first date. Her behavior, meant to entice and seduce, had just the opposite effect, because he didn't feel special by being with her. Although Deidre may very well have been "the best piece of ass" he'd had, that didn't qualify her for marriage—only sex!

Everything Old Is New

Sex alone is not going to hook a successful man. Of course, animal magnetism and chemistry is important, and sexual compatibility is a basic and necessary part of a committed relationship (although men probably consider sex much more basic and necessary than women do). Ultimately sex is nothing more than one of the many keys to intimacy.

The wise woman understands that she has to portray herself as more than just a good lay. As for a pretty face, they knew there's always competition that could top them! Just look at the images on television and videos. The girls are getting prettier, younger, and sexier. Women who marry trophy men realize that any woman can "screw his brains out," but not any woman can convince him she'd make a good wife. These women preferred to be viewed as potential wives instead of sexpots. The sexually shrewd woman realizes the difference between the two, and the difference is tremendous.

These women were presented with the difficult task of playing two roles: that of a modern adult woman who dates longer, marries later, and has needs and desires of her own versus that of the demure, discreet, "ideal wife"—sexy without being too sexual, putting out, but never putting out too much. It may sound like a schizoid role, but it's one that must be played well in order to marry the trophy man. Women who marry trophy men do not take sexual relationships lightly. They associate a certain amount of intimacy with commitment.

SECRET #11:

Loose Lips Sink Ships

HOW MANY TIMES HAVE WE HEARD THE OLD SAYING THAT it's not good to kiss and tell? Among women who marry well, it's a rule apparently well remembered and deeply understood. Although many had prior lovers before marrying their trophy men, they did not offer detailed confessions or remembrances about them. These women understood that men, no matter how successful, have certain insecurities and jealousies regarding old boyfriends. One woman said, "Only a fool tells her husband or boyfriend about her sex life with old flames. No good could come of it. Why give them details about things they already suspect? It only ends up hurting your man, and the information is guaranteed to come back to haunt you."

Trophy women are careful about confessing the number of serious boyfriends they'd had before meeting their husband, and completely close-mouthed about any sexual experience or how many men they'd had intercourse with. Allyson recalled an experience she had when her boyfriend asked her, indirectly, how many men she'd slept with. "Because I loved him, I wanted to answer truthfully, and I was naïve enough to tell him. I thought that my experience was limited—that the number was low. The fact that I really didn't have much experience apparently didn't count for much. Even worse, the fact that I'd had *any* experience at all came as a blow to him. He never got over it, and I truly believe it contributed to our breakup."

Another particularly attractive woman, previously divorced from one trophy man and married to another, said she never talked about old love with new love. "Don't let the right hand know what the left hand is doing." The new husband, she explained, knew of her old husband, but didn't really want to know the specifics. Likewise, she thought about her husband's old lovers, but knew that learning juicy details wouldn't do anybody any good. "There comes a time in a woman's life when she understands how important discretion is."

This brings us to the other side of the coin. Just as well-married women understood their trophy men didn't want to hear about other men, the women I spoke to didn't want to be the topic of hot gossip either. Although it's unfair and archaic, in many ways, a woman's reputation is the most important thing she has. One woman told us, "Shame is an emotion stronger than pride." This seems especially true among elite, upper-class Blacks, where the status and worth of a family is often judged based on the character of its women.

Even deep into well-established relationships, many women subconsciously hold back from doing anything they'd consider too risqué, deviant, or freaky. They don't consent to doing anything with a man that they'd be ashamed to have repeated or recalled. Of course, these women didn't plan on breaking up with their boyfriends, but nevertheless they didn't allow any embarrassing or vulnerable sides of their private sex lives to surface. Under no circumstances did they, for example, participate in public or group intimacy (swapping or threesomes), allow themselves to be taped or photographed doing sexually explicit things, or write revealing or compromising letters that could be read by the wrong person! Although women, unlike men, are more apt to gather and discuss intimate details about friends, family, and loved ones, they remain discreet about their sex lives. These women understood that with certain men, especially those they considered marriage material, it's best not to compromise themselves. Private life should be just that: *private.*

Similarly, the grapevine is no place to put details of your or your man's sexual preferences, innermost confessions, or arguments from the night before. Trophy men have too much to lose through careless gossip. They can't afford scandal or embarrassment. Women of substance, when intimately involved, tend to be very discreet—almost to the point of being secretive. Putting their business on public display was unheard of, so much so that even in our interviews, their answers to questions regarding intimacy and sex were closely guarded.

Madison is a nurse at a large medical clinic. She'd met an older doctor, fifteen years her senior, who'd recently joined the staff at the medical school affiliated with her clinic. In an attempt to validate their relationship and show off to the other nurses that she'd hooked this successful, older doctor, Madison began bragging and releasing a slow but continuous supply of information about this man. She'd boast about his performance in bed, how much he spent on dinner, and what their plans for the weekends were. She was excited in telling it; it made her feel as though her status among the other nurses had risen. Unfortunately, Madison didn't understand that she would have fared much better being coy, and that her man valued and expected discretion from his woman. The straw that broke the camel's back was when she started rubbing his shoulders at the nurses' station (in full view of all the probing eyes). He finally snapped when she brought her suitcase to work so they could get away early for their weekend trip. Madison had put her *and his* "bizness" in the street!

The doctor, like many trophy men, valued his privacy and didn't appreciate or condone her public displays of affection or blabber-mouthing his business. He worried that all the other nurses were snickering behind his back, and that made him feel vulnerable and silly. He'd later tell a colleague that he felt like the nurses were looking at him with X-ray glasses each time he went on the floor. Madison didn't realize her loose lips sank her own ship!

It bears mentioning that women who marry well understand that too much information about their trophy men, with other women, will cause problems. It's one thing to talk about your boyfriend, but it's another to put your business in the street. Confessions in the heat of the moment can't be taken back, and complaints can't be smoothed over. Women have memories like steel traps for salacious details. These women are careful of what they tell because they don't want it to come back to haunt them. Publicizing their personal life sparks unhealthy curiosity that might lead to contempt, jealousy, or their girlfriends' wanting to try their man for themselves. Additionally, well-married women don't risk boring their friends with weekly rehashes of "he said, she said." They don't treat their personal life like a television tabloid.

There's a difference between the confidence of friendship (for example, asking a sister or close friend for advice) and gossiping about a trophy man. Remember, telling one person something can be the same as telling hundreds. We have seen this time and time again. Who can forget the high-profile girlfriends and groupies of presidents, politicians, televangelists, and superstars? These women were the kiss-and-tell types. Did they go down in history as the bimbos or the wives? How will Monica Lewinsky be remembered?

Women who marry well rarely, if ever, discussed their sex life with other women or girlfriends. Intimate details were kept intimate. These women rarely put on public displays of sexual affection. No rubbing, groping, or hanging all over men. They considered it unladylike. These women played the part of being coy. They never casually admitted to family, coworkers, or colleagues that they slept with their trophy men. They didn't broadcast details of their love lives, and they never rehashed arguments in public. They understood that any gossip could, and would, ultimately get back to their trophy men. They've held on to the old-fashioned title of nice girl, and although they conceded that nice girls sometimes do, they've preserved their image through privacy and discretion.

Like Mother, Like Daughter, Like Wife

WE SAW REMARKABLE SIMILARITIES BETWEEN THE NURTURING and attentive upbringing our women and their trophy men received from their respective mothers.

The women who marry trophy men are indeed chips off the old block. With maturity, many women begin to become very much like their mothers. They may resoundingly protest and disagree, but like it or not, their mothers' values and beliefs are imprinted on them. This maternal influence can also be seen in other minor aspects—like the kinds of clothes a woman wears, or her hairstyle. But more important, her mother's influence also affects the men she chooses, and the way she goes about building relationships with them.

A woman who has a close relationship with her mother and family has a safety net. Trophy men admire this. Although men dread having to deal with snooping family members and nosy in-laws, they invariably appreciate a woman who has been nurtured and tutored. A girlfriend who has a close and loving relationship with her mother is likely to have been taught appropriate behavior, how to act like a lady, how to behave in public, and what's expected from a wife. It's rarely mentioned, but trophy men carefully listen to how a woman speaks of her mother, and what kind of relationship she shares with her. Close relationships, whether between man and woman or mother and daughter, share similarities, and men understand that. If a woman is quick to openly disrespect her mother, she'd be quick to openly disrespect him.

Laurel, a corporate secretary, says her husband never gave her any indication that he'd paid careful attention to her close relationship with her mom. "In fact, I sometimes worried he resented the way I put aside every Sunday to have lunch with her." But in truth, her husband felt relieved that Laurel had a close relationship with her mom. For one thing, there was a pretty good chance that Laurel, seeing how important a loving and supportive mother was, would be the same way with her own children. Children who are loved and nurtured usually grow into loving and nurturing parents, and the same can often be said about their relationships with spouses. This is a concept keenly understood by many women and especially trophy men.

This might come as a surprising secret to some of you, but don't doubt the veracity of it. I encourage you to talk openly and honestly with some of your older married girlfriends. Ask them about their early relationships with their husbands. Then ask them about their relationships with their husbands once things heated up and got serious. I am willing to bet that some aspect of the relationship was strengthened simply because the husband was impressed by his wife's interaction with his own mother, his own sisters, or small nieces or cousins in his family. Don't doubt for a minute that men are watching to see how you interact with others, and especially to see how you interact with his family. Are you gracious? Are you standoffish and self-centered? Are you overbearing? Do you try too hard? Or are you able to converse and interact in a relaxed manner and show that you are a warm, open, and receptive person?

I can think of several interesting examples. A trophy man lost his wife and suddenly found himself a single parent. The woman whom he met was quite perceptive, and willing to listen to the man's problems and help the child deal with the grief process. She didn't try to *replace* the child's mother, but helped the child work through the grief and became a sort of caregiver in the child's life. She married the widowed father sometime later.

Another example is an acquaintance who, upon first meeting her husband's family, immediately took to a tiny toddler niece. Her warm and loving interaction with the small child touched the heart of her future husband. There is some truth in the old saying that small children and animals can detect evil or ill will in people. Not only did the little child like her, she *loved* her. This only helped bolster her image in her future husband's eyes and, additionally, the rest of the family warmed to her.

A woman has a heavy cross to bear if she starts out on the wrong foot or acts standoffish or peculiar with a man's family. In a perfect world, the mother and daughter-in-law would get along. But this is not a perfect world, and sometimes it takes a lot of work and patience. Trophy women, by no means, condone rude behavior from angry or jealous mothers-in-law. In fact, quite often an angry or bitter mother-in-law can break up a new marriage. Perhaps the best footing that a woman can achieve is to first start out with a loving relationship with her own mother and allow her boyfriend, or trophy man, to see this. At least a trophy man can deduce from your own relationship with your mother that you are aware of and used to healthy loving and nurturing bonds. It would be disastrous for him to see you disparage your mother, refuse to include her in significant portions of your life, or bring a lot of excess baggage to the relationship from developmental scars and unhealthy family ties. We all know that mothers hold a wealth of knowledge; it just takes some of us longer than others to understand and appreciate that.

On a lighter note, more than one woman told me that a man who is new in a relationship and knows that one or both parents are watching him closely, if he is serious about the woman, will do his best to not mess it up. In other words, "If somebody's watching him, the chances are he is going to act better." Men who know they're going to be held accountable for their behavior (by both the woman and those who love her) might give more of an effort to doing the right thing.

However, women must be wary of telling their mothers too much about their relationships. Mothers may understand, but don't need to know too many details about boyfriend problems. If you tell her ugly and hurtful details, she'll never forget them and will harbor ill feelings toward your trophy man because, after all, she's your mother. Carla, the wife of a stockbroker, recalled that she'd once called her mom crying when a boyfriend had let her down by forgetting about her birthday. "Although now I don't regret it, it was a torpedo to the relationship. She saw how hurt I'd been, and never let me forget it. Mom couldn't stand him from then on. There's no way I could have ever made it work. Of course, who cares now, because I went on to meet my husband." The example underscores the extent of maternal influence on a relationship's longevity.

Women also must keep in mind that their mates have to be their choice. Subtle, early, and consistent psychological conditioning shaped these women's attitudes about marriage and family. The mothers of the women I spoke to empowered them and made them truly believe they deserved a good man. The women regularly, routinely, and predictably introduced their boyfriends to their mothers. They didn't want a cat in the bag. They considered sneaking around in secrecy an affront, and knew that if a relationship was cloaked in secrecy, it was unhealthy. As one woman put it, "If a man took my mother for granted, I knew he really took me and what was important to me for granted, too."

However, a mature woman must decide what's meaningful and important in her personal life. This takes greater precedence over what other people think about her, or whether or not she's been accepted because of who she dates or marries. Among these women, living up to familial expectations is important. But the wise woman understands if she primarily judges the worth of her husband and relationship by what her mother thinks of him, the marriage will be meaningless and doomed to fail. Familial or maternal approval is not the end all and be all, and nobody has to deal with your life on a day-to-day basis except for you.

A woman's relationship with her future mother-in-law is equally important. An overwhelming number of women believed their trophy men looked for many of the same characteristics in their women as they saw in their own mothers. Trophy men are often attracted to women with physical attributes similar to their mothers. Kimberly explained to us, "My husband is very focused and driven. I understood very early on that he didn't have the time or talent to teach a woman how to be a wife, a mother, or an asset. His mom was a remarkable role model, and he wanted the same kind of woman for a wife."

Well-married women often used adjectives like *healthy, looking out,* and *extremely loving* when they described the relationships between their husband and his mother. Most of the women we spoke to admired their mothers-in-law because they saw the same characteristics they found in their own moms. Even in the occasional instance when a woman didn't particularly like her mother-in-law, she'd still respect her out of deference and admiration for raising such a fantastic son. Some even went so far as to explain that despite any differences, they hoped that they could personally do as good of a job in raising their own sons or daughters.

Trophy men are often very close to and influenced by their mothers. The women who marry them understand and respect this closeness. These women were wary of any man who spoke poorly of his mother, knowing a man who disrespected his mother would disrespect them, too. Well-married women believe that loving sons make loving husbands. They understand that it's impossible to compete with a man's mother. Each person only has one mother, and it's a relationship too sacred to belittle or challenge.

It goes without saying—yet it cannot be stressed enough—that a woman should never, never belittle or malign a man's mother. It is one thing for *him* to speak ill of his mother, but you'd better believe it will raise his dander if you talk about his mom. There's a peculiar and mighty bond between a mother and her son. It doesn't matter how trifling, ridiculous, or degenerate the son is, the mother will love him until the end. And it does not matter how manipulative, sarcastic, or snoopy a mother-in-law is, the *son* will always cherish his mom. Granted, he might get disgusted with or angry at her, and see through her frailties and inadequacies, but it is one thing for him to make comments. You must never make comments.

More than a few women have told me that they have regretted saying something—in the heat of an argument or at the height of a family fray—about his mother that could not be taken back. Explained one woman, "He will hold it against you forever." It is best just to bite your tongue, even if what you have to say is true. Old people rarely change; they are set in their ways. It is a dangerous thing to assume that you are going to be the one to change someone who is stubborn and unwilling to bend.

Hideous mothers and mothers-in-law can be formidable foes. We have all heard of women who have had their eye on another young woman for their son, and would settle for nothing less. We've heard of mean old women who are intent on breaking up their sons' marriages, even if grandchildren are involved. We are not suggesting that you allow her to belittle, use, or abuse you. You have to stand up for yourself if you're personally attacked or if someone you love and cherish (your man, your children) is being challenged or endangered.

It's best to deal with a nasty mother-in-law or mother-in-law-to-be just like you would deal with a nasty coworker; ignore them and avoid them for as long as you can. Do what you can to smooth things over. Try to schedule family outings or special holidays either without her or somewhere that you know she will not be. If a woman is acerbic and nasty there may be no way that you can win her over. Avoid letting her drag you into the same type of foolishness and evil that she practices. More than one woman has told me that they have simply moved away from a neighborhood that is in close proximity to a snoopy, troublemaking mother-in-law. You have heard of the old saying "If you can't beat 'em, join 'em." Explained one wife, "I say, if you can't beat 'em, move as far away from them as you possibly can."

Meeting His Family Is the Biggest Test You'll Face—Embrace it

THE WOMEN WHO MARRIED TROPHY MEN WERE INTRODUCED to their men's families early on, and interacted with them regularly. If a man cared enough about her to introduce her to his parents, she understood the significance of this: He was serious, he cherished her, and wanted his family to know and ultimately accept her. And when the opportunity finally arose to meet his family, she was ready for it, comfortable with it, and took the occasion quite seriously.

These women understood that their trophy men's family would size them up. They submitted to this scrutiny, understanding that his family's approval was important to him. They made the extra effort to make a good impression, particularly with their man's mother.

Lindsey is a successful travel agent married to a school administrator. When her first serious boyfriend took her to meet his mom, she didn't know how to react. "At first, I was angry because I thought he'd waited too long to have me meet her. But looking back, a few months wasn't anything." Lindsey had overlooked the fact that true intimacy can't be rushed. Even worse, she then took the unrealistic view that the meeting with her boyfriend's mom was insulting. "I resented the fact that I had to gain his mother's approval. Looking back at it, his mother was very important to him, and apparently so was I. He wanted to see if we got along, and more important, if his mom approved of me. I foolishly expected him to choose between my ego, and his mom's approval. Guess who won out? His mom . . . of course!"

Lindsey can laugh about it now because she subsequently met another trophy man. The second time around, she understood the importance of meeting his mom; it was an honor, and a necessary rite of passage if the relationship was going anywhere. Thankfully, she says she got along well with her mother-in-law and made a good impression. She avoided the same self-serving, insulted attitude, and is convinced that a gracious and soft approach helped her win her husband in the long run.

Do's and Don'ts When Meeting His Family

1. Do take the meeting seriously, behaving as you would in an important interview.

2. Don't act rehearsed or contrived, because they'll see right through insincerity.

3. Do wear a simple, feminine outfit, such as a casual dress or skirt ensemble. Avoid pants.

4. Don't wear anything that appears too dressed down: casual slacks, jeans, exercise clothes, sweatsuits, or shorts.

5. Do wear simple and understated jewelry: pearl stud earrings or small gold hoops, and a simple chain.

6. Don't wear boxy, showy, glittery, or gaudy jewelry.

7. Don't, under any circumstances, call his parents by their first names (unless they specifically ask you to).

8. Do pay very close attention to your manners, answering "Yes, thank you," "No, thank you," and "please" when appropriate.

9. Don't curse or use rough phrases like "it sucks," "pissed off," or "pain in the ass."

10. Don't ask any personal questions about the family that might reveal embarrassing answers: "Where do you go to church?" (They might not attend) or "Where's your job?" (The family member might be unemployed.)

11. Do show general interest in all the family members—"How have you been?" "Are you ready for the holidays?"—and remember all their names.

12. Don't brag or boast about yourself—especially if it wasn't solicited.

13. Do explain your accomplishments if directly asked, but be modest and humble.

14. Don't volunteer unnecessary information about your mistakes or inadequacies: failed classes, bitter breakups, embarrassing tattoos, bad hair weaves, etc.

15. Don't lie about anything that can be verified (and realize that it's very likely everything you say will be verified).

16. Don't discuss sex, religion, or politics.

17. Do try to give neutral, tempered answers about current controversial news issues, if you are asked.

18. Don't divulge embarrassing personal family problems: your mother's AA chapter or your brother-in-law's jail record.

19. Do make subtle references to your relationship with your boyfriend.

20. Don't make any reference to your sexual relationship with your boyfriend, even if you've assumed his family knows you're sleeping with him.

21. Do ask questions about topics that interest his family members—that's how you get them to talk.

A word about meeting his family: Many women have asked when it is appropriate to meet a man's family. First of all, this is not something that should be suggested by the woman. If you suggest it, this might make you seem pushy or that you're way ahead of him in your relationship. However, if he ever mentions that he would like you to meet his parents, you have to be prepared to go with it. Quite often a man is not adept at selecting the most appropriate venue for this. He might want to do the right thing but is not quite aware of what is appropriate. Maybe he has never asked a girl to meet his parents before.

If you are asked for suggestions, suggest that you go to his parents' house with him, perhaps on the weekend or on a relaxed Sunday. This is always helpful because you can see from whence he came. There is a wealth of knowledge to be gained by seeing how his parents interact with each other, what his home looks like, what type of neighborhood he lived in, and how he acts around his family. If he is uncomfortable with bringing you to his house, then you could suggest a more neutral place, like Saturday lunch or Sunday brunch. Try not to make it too formal. For example, an expensive restaurant would be too stiff and stuffy, and not allow you to feel at ease. Instead, go for a casual chain-style restaurant that everyone enjoys, or perhaps even the restaurant at your local art museum. Dress to look your best and use your best manners at all times.

One particularly wise woman reminded me, "A lot of girls make the mistake of getting too loose and too comfortable around their boyfriends' parents. Early on they should act as though it's an interview, because that is exactly what it is." If you slip up or do something ridiculous, they are going to file it in their memory banks. Avoid seeming too comfortable, in other words, acting sloppy, cursing, forgetting your manners, or excessively touching him while you are with the parents. Likewise, don't order anything heavy to drink. If they are having wine or alcohol, you may have a small glass of wine, but limit yourself to only one drink. You don't want to get sloshed or say too much. Don't light up a cigarette in front of them, even if they smoke. Don't talk too much about yourself unless you are asked, and don't divulge too much about your family, especially not embarrassing anecdotes. When people are nervous, they tend to babble and say all of the wrong things, so keep your responses pertinent, well mannered, and short. Of course, this doesn't mean that you have to sit like a cigar store dummy and answer "yes" and "no" to every question. It does mean you shouldn't take things too far.

If you go to their house and you're particularly fond of the man, it would be a nice gesture to take an inexpensive gift. This could be a box of chocolates, a small coffee cake for the morning, or a bunch of beautiful fresh flowers. If the parents are known jazz or classical-music aficionados, give them a tried-and-true classic CD. None of these things cost very much, and it doesn't look like you are trying to buy their friendship. For heaven's sake, don't take any expensive gifts. The most you should spend on a gift, in this situation, should be no more than you would spend on a CD.

A lot of women caution against building relationships with your trophy man's family members, at least early in the relationship. There is an inherent danger to this. You might look as though you are trying to come on too strong, to both the trophy man and to the family members. A lot of men will use sisters or family members as double agents, to see what information they can extract from you, and this is an unfortunate trap you don't want to fall into. Additionally, it is not unheard of to build strong friendships with a boyfriend's sister or cousin and then break up with the boyfriend later. This just makes for uncomfortable, miserable feelings when people are expected to choose sides or want to reminisce about what could have been. It is also unhealthy to hang on too long after a broken relationship by asking his relatives about what the trophy man is doing now that you are no longer together.

On the other hand, if you are well established in the relationship or engaged, there is nothing wrong with embracing the family members, because they will indeed ultimately be part of your family. Some women have been brave enough to call the trophy man's mom just to see how she is doing. This is advisable only if you and she have formed a solid relationship. Otherwise, his mother might wonder, "What's she calling me for? Is she up to something? Is she trying to win me over?"

Quite often men have lifelong friends that are just as close as their family members. It's a good sign when a man wants to introduce you to his friends—you'd better believe that he's relying on them to assess you and give him feedback. Don't let your guard down, certainly don't flirt with any of them, and don't try too hard to win them over. Just be yourself and if asked, do concede that you are quite close with their friend. You should avoid telling any intimate details to his friends, no matter how relaxed and friendly they are with you, just as you should be careful about divulging too many personal secrets to his family.

She's Called a "Mother-in-Law" Because She Lays Down the Law

Fasten your seat belts, boys. It's going
to be a bumpy night.

—BETTE DAVIS, *ALL ABOUT EVE*

SOME THINGS ARE SO WEIRD THEY ALMOST DEFY EXPLANATION. This is the case when learning how to deal with your mother-in-law. Daughters-in-law seem to share a "secret sisterhood" with other women who have mothers-in-law. Some trophy men have wonderful mothers; open and loving and welcoming, the kind of woman who appreciates your love of her son. These are the kinds of women who treat you as though you were their own daughter. But others have a *serious* ax to grind because you've "swooped up" their beloved little junior.

The two biggest problems that might arise in the interaction with your mother-in-law are that *she underestimates you,* or *you underestimate her.* Either way, it's pretty foolish, and such miscommunication should be avoided at all cost.

Let's peek into two scenarios. You've met the man of your dreams. He's as smart as the late Thurgood Marshall, looks like a young Muhammad Ali, is loaded like Michael Jordan, has a sense of humor like Spike Lee, carries himself like Colin Powell, hits a golf ball like Tiger Woods, sings like the late Billy Eckstein, and is in the running for the next Nobel prize. You get the picture? He's a serious trophy man. (Remember, this is just make-believe.)

Scenario one: Things have been going pretty well between you and Mr. Trophy, and he *finally* invites you over to meet his mom and dad. You expect the elders to be trophies, too. Silly girl! You have absolutely no idea what's in store for you. After you take the first few steps into the living room, Trophy Man's parents come to meet you. For the life of you, you believe you've slipped into some sort of strange dream and his dad is the manifestation of General Colin Powell. Father Trophy is glorious. He's huge. He's dignified. He's glorious. His booming voice sounds like it's coming over a loudspeaker. You become aware of the feet at the end of your legs, but you can't explain why they suddenly feel as though they belong to somebody else, or why they're glued to the floor—preventing you from moving!

Just when you think it couldn't get any more intimidating, Mother Trophy walks over wearing her Chanel suit and puts her hand on your shoulder. Her expression looks like she smells something bad. Could that be? She speaks to you, but you hear nothing. She's looking so closely at you, you worry that you accidentally have spinach stuck in your teeth, or your skirt is unzipped, or a pink sponge curler is left in the back of your head. (You get the picture.) Just as you are certain that you're going to faint, a nervous voice from your mouth (surely not your own) floats up over the room and says, in the most immature and ridiculous manner, *"Hi, Gladys. I'm sure glad you finally had the chance to get together!"*

Scenario two: You've met the man of your dreams, and you

hope like hell that you'll get married one day in the future. He's just been promoted to manager at a major pharmaceutical company, and will soon be transferred. It breaks your heart to entertain the thought that this man, tall, dark, handsome, articulate, classy, and just plain nice, may slip though your fingers. You've reached that fork in the road, and since things have been pretty serious, he invites you to his mom's house. Things just may work out. You're eager, frantic even, to make a good impression and clinch a commitment before he moves on without you.

Because *he* is so wonderful, you naturally assume *she* will be wonderful, also. You walk into her living room, fully expecting to see Leontyne Price, or Anita Hill, or Condoleezza Rice, or Marion Anderson, or Lena Horne—but instead you see an aging Little Kim! *Or so you assume.* You'd never expected the tight lizard-skin stretch pants, the rhinestone eyeglass chains, and fading tattoo with several names crossed out, or the filterless cigarette tucked behind her ear. A James Brown album is thumping in the background, although you'd hoped for Duke Ellington or Vivaldi. You didn't expect to be served Jell-O either. She looks at you, and sees right through your disappointment and self-centered judgment. You are so aghast that you don't notice your boyfriend's shoulders slump, or the cartoon bubble above Mamma Trophy's head that's saying, "Who does this little snob think she is?"

Although the two scenarios are different yet equally ridiculous, they both underscore an important point. In the first case, the mother-in-law jumped to conclusions and misjudged the eager girlfriend. In the second scenario, the foolish girlfriend prematurely judged the trophy man's mother. Either way, somebody made the grave mistake of starting off on the wrong foot and setting the stage for future problems. *Big* problems.

A wise woman understands the precious bond between a man and his mother. You are not going to change it, nor do you have any business trying to. Women who find themselves in ulti-matum situations, where they demand, "You must choose between her and me!" set up a situation destined for failure. If a woman has to issue an ultimatum (be it because of another woman, or his mother) then she has lost control. When it gets to that ultimatum level, the girlfriend/wife has already lost the battle.

A mother is proud of her son, especially if he's a trophy man. She values and cherishes him, and naturally wants the best for him. She is just as protective of her children as *you will be of yours.* As hard as it may be for you to accept, you have to bear the bur-den of proving your worth to the protective mother. She didn't pick you, Trophy Man did. And although I'm not suggesting that you kowtow, or mindlessly suck up to a mean mother-in-law, you *do* have to give an honest effort to show her that you mean well by her son.

It's important to remember that the typical trophy man is strongly bonded with his mom. Remember, these guys are the type who make sure their "little old mommy" is well taken care of in her older years, that she's not put in any dangerous situations, that she's not short on money when she's widowed, old, and gray. A mother-in-law is a lot like a stepchild (if your trophy man just happens to already have kids) because she's going to be in your trophy man's life forever. She was there *before* you, and she might be there well *after* you.

Never allow her to unfairly judge you. Make sure she gets to know you for who you are, not just the smiling image on her son's arm who shows up on holidays or fancy parties. Likewise, don't you *dare* judge her, at least until you really get to know her as a person. If you think she's bad, how bad can she be, when she raised her son to be the object of your love and affection? She must have done *something* right, surely a fantastic job, to have borne and raised a trophy man. You agree on that, at least.

Many relationships between daughters-in-law and mothers-in-law are healthy and loving. Several important characteristics surfaced again and again when interviewing the wives of trophy men. These women were open and receptive to showing their best sides and giving their best effort to making his family seem like her family!

1. Don't disrespect your boyfriend's mother. She's not one of the girls; she's the mother of the man you love.

2. Don't ever call your boyfriend's mother by her first name, until she asks you to do so. Even then, don't get so loose or comfortable that you forget she's his mom.

3. Don't start off on the wrong foot by complaining to her about your boyfriend; although she might act like she sympathizes, she will ultimately take sides with him. After all, he's her son, right?

4. Don't embarrass yourself by trying to buy her affection with expensive gifts. It will only backfire on you.

5. Don't dare judge her. Who the hell do you think you are? Really, so what if she wears a housecoat or a hair net, or she's not the television image you expected? She was good enough to raise her son, right? You also have to remind yourself, should you have kids, she's the grandmother!

6. Do ask her for advice about certain matters as long as they are not related to her son. For example, show her that you'd like to learn something she's good at (a certain craft), or ask her what she thinks about a new fad, or what life was like

when she was a girl. (Be careful, don't get too familiar too soon and ask questions she might feel are embarrassing. Instead, ask questions that allow you to see what her life is all about. Everybody's mom was once a young girl with hopes, dreams, and ambitions of her own.) You can learn a great deal about her, as well as your man's feelings, by simply listening to your future mother-in-law.

7. Do give it your best effort to remain well mannered and thoughtful whenever you're around her. She's watching.

8. Do dress like a lady when you're around her. She's taking note.

9. Do make your best concerted effort to get along, should you marry your trophy man. Learn the meaning of the saying "Let it go." If you find yourself in a sensitive situation with your mother-in-law then you "click," beautiful! If you don't, and you can honestly say that you've given it your best shot, move yourself and your husband. You can go about your lives without quarreling or the stress that so often accompanies family matters when folks don't get along.

"Can't we all just get along?"

Men Don't Want to Marry Divas

IT'S NO SECRET THAT THE WOMEN WE INTERVIEWED HAD attitude. By *attitude*, I don't mean that they were uppity, snobbish, or self-centered, but rather they had an air about them that oozed self-esteem. But there is an important difference between self-esteem and egotism. We all know the egotist who checks her reflection each time she passes a window or mirror, brags about the zillion men who want her, never goes an hour without fixing her hair, and sleeps in a full face of makeup. We can't stand her, and neither can men. The egotist is a woman who has, unfortunately, confused self-love with being egocentric. She's a diva, and trophy men avoid divas.

Divas are usually too absorbed in their own appearance, their own needs, and busy boasting that they don't have to please anybody but themselves to build a meaningful relationship with anybody. A bitch continually asks, "What's in it for me?" We all know the prima donnas, who meet a man and immediately want to know what he can do for them. A woman named Chantal made a good point. "I've had girlfriends who expected, and even asked boyfriends to pay for their hair and nail appointments.

They figured if a man wanted them to look good, he'd better pay for it. I could never do that, and never asked my husband to pay for anything personal while we dated. It seemed like something a prostitute would do. Totally sleazy."

A wise woman understands that she is judged by what she does, not what she says. There's an old saying, "I heard what you *said*, but I'm watching *what you do*." Trophy men notice if a woman does nothing but spend countless hours at the beauty salon. They're turned off by vain, selfish, or indifferent behavior. They can smell a self-centered woman like a hunting dog, and find it distasteful. Why? It's obvious. Can you make a life with someone who is only thinking about herself?

Contrast this with the women who married trophy men. These women understood that being attractive has nothing to do with being self-serving. They were too busy, too successful, and too focused to spend countless hours at the gym, the beauty salon, or the masseuse. Instead of living at the gym or the beauty salon, these women spent more of their time concentrating on their interests, their personal growth, and their relationships. The women we interviewed had too much self-esteem to ask boyfriends to be responsible for their grooming. Because they cared about themselves, they'd never cheapen their self-esteem by using it as barter.

The women I spoke with made it clear that they were willing to compromise and meet men halfway on issues involving serious long-term planning. They would move to another city if the man committed to them and the move helped his career. They would move to a neighborhood if it benefited their man and considered what impact these major expenses would have for their future. They didn't risk alienating their trophy men with selfish behavior, and their trophy men felt comforted by their mates' willingness to make sacrifices on their behalf.

The women who married trophy men knew that inflexibility in a relationship—especially on the woman's part—will make that relationship snap.

Being Nice

Well-married women placed a good deal of emphasis on acting nice. As a group, they were well educated, attractive, and ambitious, and despite all the reasons they had to act snooty, they approached the men they admired or wanted very carefully. They were proud to describe themselves as "sweet," "easygoing," and "understanding" toward their men when they first met them. All seemed to intuitively understand that men, especially driven and successful men, are putty in the hands of a woman they consider soft and sweet. Such views didn't seem sexist to them, and they certainly didn't consider going out of their way to appear kind as a show of weakness. They simply realized that the men they were dating had enough of a challenge at their jobs and didn't need or want their relationship or love affair to be just another difficult, stressful challenge to add to the heap.

Brittany, who is married to a television personality, says, "Who wants a bitch? That hard, corporate persona may be okay if you're a criminal lawyer, or conducting a company meeting, but men sure in the heck don't want it in their love life. I went out of my way to show him how sweet I was—told him how much I loved the restaurant he first took me to and told him honestly how thrilled I was that he telephoned me. He didn't see this as eager or frantic. He just considered it sweet. He ate it up."

Kalyn is married to a prominent engineer. She hit the nail on the head by explaining a simple fact to me. "Everybody remembers that old Janet Jackson song called "What Have You Done for Me Lately?" Although it was a nice dance song, the attitude has no place in a serious and potentially loving relationship. Women who are always looking for a better deal from the next man stand out like a red flag in the middle of the snow. If a man senses a snarling, bitchy, demanding, and self-serving attitude, he will drop her like a hot potato.

It's amazing how much mileage you can get out of a little bit of sweet behavior. Nobody likes a hard-edged surly witch except perhaps as a fictional television character.

A clinical professor recalled making homemade oatmeal-raisin cookies for her boyfriend to snack on when he had a hard weekend or late night at the office while preparing for an important presentation. When asked why she just didn't buy them or have them delivered, she answered, shocked, that he loved homemade treats. At the time she was a medical resident. She could have spent her leisure time on a dozen more pressing issues, but the gesture was quite symbolic; it seemed sweet and awfully nice. She's convinced that small acts of kindness such as this helped her win over her trophy man. Behaving nicely is considered equally as important as looking pretty.

In a marriage, a couple must depend on each other and anchor each other. That willingness gives tremendous strength to trophy couples. Quite often, the woman a trophy man decided to marry was the one most willing to motivate him and encourage him when nobody else would.

The women I spoke with complimented their men, and spent time stroking their egos. They didn't dwell on their inadequacies but instead reminded them that they're special. They praised what was good about the men, but never lied or made things up. The wise woman understands successful men are a "package" of years of hard knocks and disappointment mixed with success; good times mixed with bad times. Combine this with the fact that successful men often downplay and hide failures, disappointments, and regrets, and we begin to see the critical role these women play as allies. As one well-married woman joked, "I know that if I don't take good care of him, another woman will."

Well-married women spoiled their trophy men when they were dating. They remembered details like favorite meals, thoughtful (but not expensive) gifts, and handwritten notes when they weren't expected. Likewise, these women play along with wifely or womanly behavior—role-playing that's harmless and bolsters his male ego (for example, taking him chicken soup when he's sick or helping select his secretary's Christmas gift).

Women married to trophy men were also careful, however, when it came to doing nice little things for their boyfriends. There is a difference between doing what is appreciated and appropriate, and taking it too far. On a humorous note, I don't know too many women who actually enjoy doing their own laundry or cleaning their own house. So why in the world would a girlfriend go out of her way to do serious housecleaning or laundry for her boyfriend? Sure, if he's sick, if he has recently experienced the death of a family member, or there's been some other extenuating circumstance and he needs help, it's only right for you to get in there and push up your sleeves. But if you're talking about routinely cleaning up for a man or doing his laundry, you end up presenting yourself as a maid, not a girlfriend. The other sad truth is the more you do, the more you'll do. You know exactly what I mean. If you have a busy and active life of your own, why in the world would you take all your free time to devote to cleaning up after a man? Don't do it.

Now, there will be some idiotic sisters who'll take this to an extreme and not lift a finger, ever. It is perfectly normal, for example, to go to his house for dinner and help wash the dishes afterward, or stack pots and pans. In fact, that is good manners. Another example would be if you have a small party and entertain together, you could help with setting the refreshments, getting the stereo booted up, and tidying up afterward. This type of thing is not only acceptable, but also expected in someone who has good manners and good sense.

Trophy men by nature are busy, goal-oriented, and motivated. Therefore, it is no surprise they rise to the challenge when they meet a woman they are interested in. But, on the other hand, if a woman plays the old hard-to-get role, it might just backfire on her. Successful men have no time for games, and because they are successful, these men dislike the idea or feeling of being rejected, especially by a woman they are interested in. If a woman acts too cute, too busy, or too in demand, she might just act herself right out of the dating game with a trophy man. Don't confuse the appearance of selectivity and tastefulness with being an outright snobbish, self-centered diva.

It's amazing how many times being nice was considered a winning point with women and their trophy men. There is no big mystery to it; men are attracted to women who treat them kindly. Unfortunately, just as with some of my other examples, there are going to be some confused women who take this nice thing too far. There is a big difference between being nice to the man and being his doormat. Women married to trophy men have a strong sense of self, and are careful not to do anything under the guise of being nice that is actually just demoralizing.

Let me give you an example that will make your hair stand on end. As hard as it may seem to believe, this example is true. I know a woman (with a lot on the ball) who was crazy about a man. He was a successful realtor and had remained a bachelor well into his early forties. He sold his town house and bought oceanfront property. Naturally, after selling the town house, he had to clean it and make it ready for the new buyers. The only problem was it had a storage attic that was literally overrun with bugs. At the risk of grossing you out, I will tell you the crawl space was reportedly filled with bug traps and roach motels that were fully occupied. Yuck! Unbelievably, this man mentioned the fact that he had all these dead bugs and fully occupied roach motels in his attic and the woman volunteered to help him clean it. Jackass that he was, he bailed out at the last minute and let her do the job alone on a Saturday morning. I don't know which is more disgusting—the fact that he would allow her to do it or that she agreed to do it. Certainly, he lost any trophy-man status by letting a woman, or any friend for that matter, clean up his dead-bug mess instead of doing it himself. Clearly, this is an example of when being too nice is just being dumb.

The well-married women overwhelmingly disapproved of playing hard to get, or staging self-serving "scenes" to provoke jealousy or admiration in their trophy men. They understood that spontaneous and sincere acts of kindness would go a lot further than behaving like a self-centered wretch.

SECRET #16:

Be Independent, But
Let Him Be a Man

WOMEN MARRIED TO TROPHY MEN REALIZE THE IMPORTANCE of letting a man be a man. Before the feminists among us get our hackles up, let me explain the subtlety of this secret. Underneath the gruff and tough exterior, men are quite often just as sensitive, if not more so, than women. Through no fault of their own they have been led to believe they must live up to a certain "manly" image. Completely secure men will sometimes feel challenged if they somehow feel their role *as a man* is questioned. Even the smallest little things, like a woman hurrying to open the door for herself, insisting she open her own car door, or refusing his help with her coat, are sometimes seen as an affront to a man's ego. Even if you don't need his help, it is always gratifying for a man to think that you do—at least a little bit. These women did not demand psychiatric counseling and support (in other words, telling him all of your problems), nor did they demand financial support or expect him to make all of the important decisions in their lives. They made these decisions on their own. However, consulting him, asking him for his opinions, bolstering his role as the man in their life, all help to nurture a relationship and make him feel valued.

Nothing drives a man crazy quicker than a woman who answers each and every question he asks her with "I want to do whatever you want to do." This can be a simple question about a restaurant: "*Where would you like go to dinner?*" and the girlfriend answers, "*Wherever you want to go.*" "*What movie would you like to see?* And the girlfriend answers, "*I want to see whatever you want to see.*" Or how about even more important issues: "*What neighborhood do you think we should buy our first house in?*" And she answers, "*I want to move wherever you want to move.*"

If you've ever had the pleasure of seeing *Coming to America,* the Eddie Murphy movie about an African prince who marries an American sweetheart, there's a funny scenario where the prince meets a young African princess who has been groomed for marriage. She has no mind of her own and answers every question he poses with "I want what you want." To test how far her devotion to him stretches, he asks her to hop on one foot like a monkey and, sure enough, she does it. Get the picture?

Independent, desirable women have minds of their own, have plans and desires of their own, and don't live solely through their men. The same goes with their finances. They have their own income, their own savings, and their own long-term plans. These women shied away from men who seemed shaky and unable to support themselves or even do simple things like pay for dates.

Women who married trophy men had their personal finances in order well before they married or met their trophy men. These women had their own savings accounts, checking accounts, retirement accounts, and investments. In other words, they were completely self-supporting. Some even had wills and impressive long-term financial plans and portfolios.

These women did not ask their trophy men for money. Even if the man was wealthy, they assumed nothing. These were not the kinds of women who expected, suggested, or asked their boyfriends to pay for hairdresser appointments, manicures, or special outfits for special occasions. These women didn't ask, under any circumstances, for their trophy men to pay for rent, or credit-card or car payments. They never considered their boyfriends to be banks. They didn't want to shame themselves or put their boyfriends on the spot. And a sexual relationship even deepened their refusal to ask boyfriends for money. They didn't want to imply a sex-for-money situation. They considered such behavior cheap, and more appropriate of a call girl. Remember, the goal is to be considered wife potential, not simply girlfriend material.

At the same time, they knew that a successful man wants to showcase his success. He needs to feel as if he can give something to a woman he's interested in. Knowing this, the women I interviewed rarely if ever paid for dates with their trophy men. These women appreciated chivalry, expected men to behave honorably, and didn't settle for less. Cathleen, an owner of a small catering business who's married to a systems analyst, explained, "I think the women's movement and women's lib has really messed up a lot of people. Sure, I agree a woman should get paid equally for equal work. But I don't want a man to stop treating me special when I'm involved with him. I'm his woman, not his buddy. Both of us know I have a job and my own money. But it would cheapen things, leave me feeling disappointed, if he asked me, or expected me, to pay for dates."

Authentic trophy men don't want their women to pay for dates. A trophy man would consider it an affront to sit at a dinner table with a waiter hovering about as his woman fished around for her credit card. These are often old-fashioned men, honorable types, who enjoy pampering their girlfriends and wives.

Several women admitted to having insisted on picking up the check with old boyfriends in the past. And in hindsight, they considered it a mistake. They said they regretted it the moment they'd done it; resented the cost, and the fact that the man allowed it, and dreaded the possibility that he might expect them to pay again. One woman took the caustic view that a man who couldn't truly afford to ask her on a date had no business asking her, period.

Routinely paying for dates sets a bad precedent. But all the women we interviewed did cover expenses for special occasions every once in a while. They would treat if it were the man's birthday or if they were celebrating his job promotion. Or they orchestrated a special home-cooked dinner or small gathering rather than paying for an expensive date.

There's a fine line between allowing a man to play his masculine role, and acting like you are making him bear the weight of everything. It is important to find ways to behave so the trophy man doesn't find you selfish. One woman, who was dating a busy systems analyst, would help in date planning. She explained,

> During the week, I knew he was busy at work and had important deadlines to meet. The weekends were really the only times that we could get together, especially since we lived clear across town from each other. I would help out by doing the research and planning behind our dates. For example, I would make it my business to get the newspaper toward the end of the week and see which cinemas were playing what movies, which affordable restaurants were in the area, or which seasonal fairs or repertory concerts or plays were being conducted. It helped quite a bit for me to have firm suggestions with time and place when Friday would roll around and he would ask, "What do you think we should do?" I could give him several options, and as long as I took care not to make things too extravagant, he

*usually appreciated me taking the reins in helping plan our
weekend.*

Other examples include helping him to shop for things like
Mother's Day gifts, birthday gifts for his sisters, or things that he
may otherwise be left totally confused as to which to choose.
Another woman we know helped her boyfriend with selecting
decorations for his new condo. She laughs as she explains, "It was
really quite fun. I knew that I had a better understanding of fabrics, furniture, and what went with what. He couldn't quite yet
afford an interior decorator, and he was unsure about fashions
and a style for the town house himself. I didn't take over, but I did
enjoy going along with him to browse through furniture stores,
go into the curtain outlet stores, and the rug warehouses, to help
him piece together a nice, new, masculine apartment. It was a
learning experience for both of us, and I think he really appreciated it."

All of us know the difference between an *acquaintance, just
a friend,* and a *real friend.* In other words, there are certain people
whom we know we can depend on, when we're moving, to come
over and help pack boxes. There are certain people we know we
can depend on to pick us up at the airport at an odd time after a
long business flight. And there are certain people we can count
on to stand by us when the chips are down. This is the type of
friend you should be to your trophy man. The importance of
being both a girlfriend, and yet a *real friend,* cannot be stressed
too much. A real friend is someone who stands by you through
thick and thin, knows when to pull back and not be overbearing
or suffocating, and knows when it is important to consider other
people besides him- or herself.

Being a Housewife and/or Mother Can Be the Toughest Career You'll Ever Love

SOMEWHERE ALONG THE WAY IN THE PAST FEW DECADES came the ridiculous notion that "just being a housewife" was considered somehow inferior. Women got all confused about their roles in the workforce and began to believe the hype that staying home, taking care of the house and their man and children, would somehow make them less of a woman than if they went out and pursued a "professional" career. Among many of the women whom I interviewed, I saw that nothing could be further from the truth. I have to say this secret was intriguing to me personally, because I'd fed into the hype for so long I, myself, began to believe it also. But then I met several women married to trophy men who pursued their roles as homemakers and mothers just as aggressively as some of the other sisters pursued their roles as teachers, doctors, lawyers, and businesswomen. Women have been naïve enough to believe that somehow staying at home made them less of a woman, and it has gotten so out of control that we've even started to judge other women as somehow being less of an intriguing woman because they don't work outside the home.

After interviewing several stay-at-home moms, I'm here to tell you that staying home is in many ways actually harder than going out to work. What is fascinating is that these women never considered themselves as settling for less by staying at home. These women always hoped, dreamed, and worked toward the idea of being full-time wives, just as their cohorts worked toward being professional "working women."

It is a subtle thing, the hopes and dreams of being a full-time mother or a housewife. Women are actually sometimes embarrassed or, heaven forbid, ashamed to admit that they would like to just stay at home and keep their house, man, and children together. These women are just as dedicated and goal-oriented, in some cases more so, than their career-minded counterparts. Let me give you an example of a woman married to the quintessential trophy man in southern California. He is a lawyer, and she married him somewhat later in life. She had already pursued and achieved a highly successful career as an art and antique broker. She had gone to college and networked her way through the workforce until she landed the prestigious job of her dreams. But then, just as she approached fortysomething, she decided she wanted to start a family. Fortunately, because her husband was a successful lawyer, she had the leisure (and note that I use this word wisely) of opting to stay at home and trying to start a family. She was blessed with a beautiful child and decided that the upbringing of this child superceded any of her achievements in the retail arena. Furthermore, her husband was eager for her to stay at home and devote all of her energy toward raising their child properly. Because he had the means to support her, and because she had already "been there, done that" in the workplace, she had no problem—no hesitation—in closing one chapter of her life and opening another.

Foolishly, some of her friends pitied her, assuming that she had given up a lot to just be a stay-at-home mom. Quite the contrary. She devoted countless hours every day to raising her baby daughter, watching her grow and reach developmental milestones, and then later, taking her back and forth to school, lessons, and childhood activities. There is something quite touching about being able to see your baby take her first steps, or have her first piano recital, and shuttle her back and forth to ballet lessons. This mother is careful not to judge or insinuate that working mothers somehow slight their children, because each case is very different.

She points out that devoting her time *fully* to her child and her home demands more attention than her "regular job" ever did. She also has the sense of satisfaction in knowing she is primarily responsible for the character and upbringing of her child. If anyone foolishly thinks that she gives her time only to her child, then they have missed the point. The child-rearing is, of course, the most important facet, but only one facet. This trophy woman has an impeccable house, entertains her husband's colleagues, is active in charitable organizations, and takes care to give special attention to her aging parents. She is well rounded, multifaceted, and makes no apologies for living her life the way she wants.

Another example is a trophy woman married to a pharmaceutical representative in the Midwest. She was educated—actually highly educated—in the field of engineering. She married a trophy man who was very serious about family and children. Because he was highly successful in his field, he not only wanted her to stay at home but also devote her time to the family, church, and home. She was brave enough to admit that her values lay with her home first, that she owed little to her profession, and that her man and her children were the most important things in her life. Now, many years into their marriage, she has raised three absolutely gorgeous daughters who are grounded and indicative of the kind of children who have had ready access to a loving home. The husband is indeed the man of the house, and is a stabilizing force. This trophy sister considers herself fortunate to be able to work for her family instead of working for somebody else.

The two examples just given illustrate women who have left their careers or changed their priorities from high-powered business to full-time mom. But make no mistake; there are many women who opt to bypass the "career route" altogether and dive headfirst into being a full-time wife, homemaker, and mother. These women often, though not always, married during their younger years. This is expected, especially since they were able to bypass extensive schooling and job training to go directly after their main priority of being a consummate wife, companion, mother, and homemaker.

What's fascinating about these housewives is that they approach their role with just as much tenacity, just as much gusto, as the women who pursued more corporate careers. They seem to exemplify the old saying "If you're going to do something, do it right." It's ironic that often these women are pitied by working women for being "trapped at home," yet on the flip side of the coin, these homemakers often pity the career women for running on that never-ending treadmill of the dog-eat-dog game of corporate America. Indeed, they pay just as much attention to detail in their home life as many working sisters pay in their professional lives. In other words, their home, their family, and their family's happiness is their profession. Consequently, they tend to be in very strong, loving, well defined, and nurturing positions in their household, where they are truly indispensable.

A final example typifies just such a woman. College and career just isn't for everybody—no more so than being a full-time homemaker is for everybody. The last example of the consummate homemaker is a woman out of Long Island. She married a very prestigious and high-powered lawyer, who dedicated his early, formative work years toward building up his own private practice and then law firm. After the birth of their first child, he strongly urged her to stay at home to "take care of business," and she was happy to oblige. The career route, in the strictest sense of the word, was never quite her cup of tea. However, keeping the house clean, pleasing her man, raising her daughter, and entertaining his clients were her forte. She looked at this very much as a full-time job or career and, in the truest sense of the word, she pointed out that it made more sense to make her *man* happy than making her *boss* at some company happy. She was fortunate enough to find herself in the position of not having to work outside the home, so she didn't. And once the child became of school age, her mother began to develop her own interests outside the home. The beauty of this was she only had to do as much as she wanted to. She now runs her own catering service, and although she does it for the sheer pleasure of cooking, she makes more money than she might have in a traditional corporate job.

The take-home point is as follows: If a woman relishes the role of wife, homemaker, mistress of the house, and mother, then she should pursue it as aggressively just as she would any other job. In fact, this is probably the hardest job of any of the women interviewed. It takes a steady hand and a sound mind to balance your own self-esteem and, at the same time, make sure that everyone else in the home is happy. These women would no more have a stranger raise their child or an "abbreviated" relationship with their husband than they would cut off their own hands. In many ways, the husbands seemed to appreciate the fact that they don't have to come home to a wound-up, stressed-out, spread-too-thin wife in the evening after work. They appreciated and relished coming home to a beautiful house, well-fed children, and home cooking. Don't be foolish enough to think this is an old-fashioned picture, because it is not. These women opt to do this just as others opt to do other things with their lives. There is nothing less or more admirable about one choice or the other. Their roles are usually well defined—and defined primarily by the woman, and not the husband. Because it works for the wife, it works for the whole family.

Final Word

TROPHY MEN, LIKE GOLDEN OPPORTUNITIES, JUST DON'T walk up to a woman's door and knock. They're not lounge lizards that you meet at bars or dance clubs or through classified ads. And you don't lock eyes with them over a pile of vegetables in the produce department at the grocery store. Meeting a trophy man is difficult enough, and sustaining a relationship with him can sometimes be a challenge. You've met his family and they adore you. He's met your family and they adore him. Is the next step a walk down the aisle? If you've followed the advice in this book, marriage is probably around the corner. It might happen.

One of the most important concepts our women understood was the universal notion of a man's readiness to commit. Every single man—young, old, rich, poor, black, or white—knows the concept of "readiness." A man is not going to marry until he's ready. The women who marry trophy men know it, understand it, and deal with it accordingly. They understood that in order to marry a trophy man, they had to meet him at a time in his life when he was emotionally ready and receptive to marrying. Of course, the couple has to love each other, because without love none of the other stuff matters. But all these women either knew girlfriends who'd had loving boyfriends who'd refused to commit, or they themselves had been in genuine love affairs that led nowhere. Quite often (among other complex issues) the time just wasn't right. A man's "readiness factor" is of utmost importance, especially if he has spent his life on the fast track—in school, developing his business or molding his career.

Never debase yourself by forcing the timing. None of the women we spoke with gave their boyfriends marriage ultimatums. None proposed to the man. Not one well-married woman interviewed used an accidental pregnancy to trap her trophy man. Of course, this trickery undoubtedly still occurs, but a shotgun marriage is a bad beginning—it's desperate, stale, selfish, and doomed to fail. Many women gently explained that (perhaps unfairly or unrealistically) out-of-wedlock pregnancies were viewed by their men as hallmarks of poor and lower-class women, or out-of-touch movie stars. If a man didn't want to commit to a woman for herself, he certainly didn't want to commit or settle because of an unplanned or unwanted child. To quote one woman, "If a man didn't want me, why would he want my child?"

Don't settle for cohabitation either. Most of the women did not live with their trophy man before marriage, fearing that living together would ruin any chance of marriage later. If they did live together, they did so for less than six months before getting married, often to save money for the wedding and reception.

It may seem that being in the right place at the right time to get married is all up to fate. But not so, not so at all. Some parameters of the "right time and right place" are controllable, and we've seen how trophy women control them.

Skeptics may second-guess a woman's chances of meeting and marrying a trophy man if she's somehow not "hooked up." It is difficult to negotiate your way into the inner circle without time, connections, and money. But my research revealed surprising secrets that any woman, anywhere, can apply to her life. What worked for one woman might very well work for many. All women can emulate the ways that well-married women carried themselves, pursued education, consulted their family, secured their own financial stability, and met men.

Most of the women we spoke with adhered to good old-fashioned common sense, self-honesty, and diligence for their own goals. Their lives and husbands give credence to their observations and advice. Many of the surprising secrets are simply time-honored values, familiar traditions, and methods that have always set apart the upper class from others. They didn't *return* to classic standards and behavior. They never *strayed from* that behavior.

Here's a review of the top ten characteristics of women married to trophy men.

1. **They had a career and financial stability of their own.** Women married to trophy men are usually trophies themselves. They weren't looking to be saved. These women often had exciting and prestigious jobs that provided them with financial stability. They never, ever asked their boyfriends for money or financial favors. In fact, these women looked disparagingly at "sugar daddies."

2. **They were, for the most part, educated.** Women married to trophy men were usually educated, often more educated than the men. All finished high school, the vast majority finished college, and many received postgraduate degrees. They pursued education for themselves and quite often met the trophy man in the process. And because these women were educated, they tended to marry and have babies at later ages—when they were much wiser, patient, and personally secure.

3. **They had strong religious beliefs and convictions.** Women married to trophy men relied on

their spiritual strength when making decisions at the crossroads of their lives. They were not afraid of letting their man see their religious side, and they believed he respected them more because of it.

4. They are family-centered. Women married to trophy men often came from strong family backgrounds. Their mothers were also married to trophy men. Consequently, maternal influence played a tremendous role in teaching and grooming these women's behavior and standards, both directly and subconsciously.

5. They are familiar with well-married role models. Women married to trophy men knew strong and loving couples from their family and group of friends. These couples provided an example to follow, and gave advice to the women during their formative years, and later in adulthood when dating serious boyfriends. Having a real (instead of perceived) foundation for comparison allowed these women to make wise and pragmatic decisions regarding their trophy men. Our research showed that well-married women understood and lived by these surprising secrets. Many other women would do well understanding the reality of these concepts, because once understood, the trophy man can be theirs.

6. They worked at looking their best. Women married to trophy men are, for the most part, average-looking. They are not ravishing beauty queens. Even if they were above average, simply taking measures to enhance their looks made all the difference. They did not resort to expensive hair weaves, fake fingernails, or outrageous boob

jobs, but rather eating healthy, keeping their weight under control, learning how to use makeup, and dressing in classic clothes made the difference. Subtle changes create the biggest impact.

7. They worked incredibly hard at being nice. Women married to trophy men believed their niceness and kindness accounted for more than any other attribute in winning over their trophy man. This not only included her treatment of him personally, but also how she treated others in his presence.

8. They were sexually shrewd. Women married to trophy men didn't have sex too soon or too easily at the beginning stages of their relationship. They didn't use sex for barter. They didn't try to entrap men into shotgun marriages with accidental pregnancy. And above all, they understood the double standard held by men in wanting "nice, wife-material" women without too much past sexual history or experience.

9. They didn't pressure their man into marriage. Women married to trophy men didn't nag or pressure them into proposing. They accepted the fact that men won't marry until they're ready. They waited until he was ready to propose, and cut their losses and moved on when they sensed they were being strung along. They understood that relationships required a certain amount of traditional role-playing, and often let the man at least believe he was making the important decisions.

10. They learned from prior love affairs. Women married to trophy men kissed a few frogs to get

to their prince. They didn't fool themselves with the myths of love at first sight or "He should love me and my faults unconditionally." Old mistakes were not repeated and dirty laundry or hurtful details were never repeated.

I had a wise old teacher who used to say, "The last thing I say will be the main thing you remember." I've tried to be concise in presenting you the messages about trophy men, directly from the messengers who are married to them. Hopefully, you will have pulled out a few skills that you can personally apply to your own life. Some tried-and-true rules of thumb will also help you in making wiser decisions in your relationships. Indeed, what has been written is true. The names have been changed, perhaps, to protect the innocent (and the guilty), but they are real-life stories that we can all relate to.

You're at the airport. You see a couple with two small boys. They are attractive, and something about them seems different. He could be a little taller, she could be a little thinner, but they both seem comfortable and at ease with themselves and each other. They are a beautiful couple, and you can tell they've been working on it. They are calm and happy as they get on their flight. The two small children are dressed neatly, identically, and follow with manners and self-assuredness that's unusual for such small children. Somewhere behind them, a grandparent or a nanny follows closely. The couple is deep in conversation with each other, talking about work, the flight schedule, and where they might have a chance to have dinner together once they've reached their point of destination. He's wearing khakis and a sports coat; she's in a wrap dress from the Gap, complete with nice jewelry and a designer bag.

You look at yourself and think, She's got it made. She has a husband, cute kids, and the money to be traveling with a nanny.

Hopefully, after reading this book, you are able to *see what is not there*. You should now realize that they knew each other back when neither had a pot to pee in. They opened their own business together and, at the end of the day, would shut the doors and clean the bathrooms and toilets themselves. Sure, they have money to fly first class now, but there was a time when they drove secondhand cars cross country to make it through college. The marriage of ten years has been a process in evolution—not all roses, but certainly based on love, mutual admiration, and determination. You don't see all of the responsibility and sacrifice they have had to deal with. You don't see the bad times along with the good. You don't see what it took to finally make things work.

Let me give you another example. There is a golden couple that lives on the East Coast. They have two beautiful daughters in the best of private schools. He is a successful professional; she is the lady who runs the business. They have a beautiful house that overlooks the bay, drive fancy cars, and take exotic vacations to places like Monaco. Anyone in his or her right mind would look at them and say, "Boy, they've got it made."

But once again, after reading this book, you will *hopefully see what is not there*. You'd see how they met, how they had to go through the intricacies of making the relationship work. You'd see how she's had to focus a lot of her energy on the business and family and put some of her hopes and dreams on hold. You'd see how he's had a long and methodical job of building up his business before he was named one of the best professionals in the entire state. They finally got there, but it hadn't always been an easy ride.

These are true stories, because I know the women well. Although the pictures might be slightly different, the message has always been the same. All of the women married to trophy men had much to offer and have learned much in the process of seeking love and marriage. They had their own careers, hopes, and dreams; they were either highly educated or highly motivated; and they were grounded in some sense of spirituality or belief. They all learned from prior experience and impressions from long-married couples (often within their own families). They worked hard at maintaining family, peace of mind, and happiness in their homes. They're women just like you. It is the ultimate proof that you, too, can have a trophy man.

List of African-American Yearly Social Events

Take care to get what you like, or you will be
forced to like what you get.

—GEORGE BERNARD SHAW

JANUARY

Professional Women of Color
P.O. Box 4572
New York, NY 10185
212-714-7190
PWCinsight@aol.com

FEBRUARY

Black Enterprise & AXA/Equitable Ski Challenge
130 Fifth Ave.
New York, NY 10011
800-209-7229
hsutt@advantageintl.com

The College Fund/UNCF's National Alumni Council
Conference
8260 Willow Oaks Corp. Dr.
Fairfax, VA 22031
MQuidley@UNCF.org

National Association of African American Studies
Morehead State University
212 Rader Hall
Morehead, KY 40351
606-783-2650
1.berry@morehead-st.edu

The Black Engineer of the Year Awards Conference
729 E. Pratt St., Suite 504
Baltimore, MD 21202
410-244-7101
www.ccgmag.com

The African American Student Union of the Harvard
Business School
2405 HBS Student Mail Center
Boston, MA 02163

National Minority Business Council
235 E. 42nd St.
New York, NY 10017
212-997-4753
Fax: 212-997-5102
NMBC@msn.com

National Brotherhood of Skiers
1525 East St., Suite 402
Chicago, IL 60615
773-995-4100
www.nbs.org

March

UCLA's African American Leadership Institute
110 Westwood Plaza, Suite A 101d
Los Angeles, CA 90095
310-825-2001
execed@anderson.ucla.edu

National Association of Black-Owned Broadcasters
1333 New Hampshire Ave., Suite 1000
Washington, DC 20036
202-463-8970
nabob@abs.bet

Harvard Black Law Students Association
1541 Massachusetts Ave.
Cambridge, MA 02138
617-495-4556
dmccray@lw.harvard.edu

University of Pennyslvania Black Law Students
    Association
3400 Chestnut St.
Philadelphia, PA 19104
215-898-9370

National Society of Black Engineers
1454 Duke St.
Alexandria, VA 22314
703-549-2207
www.nsbe.org

International Black Buyers & Manufacturers Expo
    & Conference
312 Florida Ave. NW
Washington, DC 20001

202-797-9070
www.IBBMEC.com

MOBE/Marketing Opportunities in
    Black Entertainment
6 N. Michigan Ave., Suite 909
Chicago, IL 60602
773-651-8008
raimobe@aol.com

Student National Medical Association, Inc.
1012 10th St. NW
Washington, DC 20001
202-882-2881

National Association of Black College Broadcasters
P.O. Box 3191
Atlanta, GA 30302
404-523-6136

April

National Association of Black Social Workers
8436 W. McNichols St.
Detroit, MI 48221
313-862-6700

National Coalition of Black Meeting Planners
8630 Fenton St., Suite 126
Silver Spring, MD 20910
202-628-3952
NCBMP@compuserve.com

American Association of Blacks in Energy
927 15th St. NW, Suite 200
Washington, DC 20005

202-371-9530
aabe@erols.com

National Conference of Black Mayors, Inc. (NCBM)
1422 W. Peachtree St. NW, Suite 800
Atlanta, GA 30309
404-765-6444

National Association of Black Telecommunications
    Professionals, Inc. (NABTP)
1710 H St. NW, 10th Floor
Washington, DC 20006
800-946-6228
www.NABTP.org

Black Management Association J. L. Kellogg Graduate
    School of Management
Northwestern University
2001 Sheridan Rd.
Evanston, IL 60208
847-441-3939

National Association of Health Services Executives
    (NAHSE)
8630 Fenton St., Suite 126
Silver Spring, MD 20910
202-628-3953
NAHSE@compuserve.com

National Alliance of Market Developers (NAMD)
P.O. Box 4666 Rockefeller Station
New York, NY 10185
namdntl@earthlink.net

National Black Flight Attendants of America, Inc.
1060 Crenshaw Blvd.

Los Angeles, CA 90019
323-299-3406

MAY

Black Enterprise/Nations Bank Entrepreneurs
    Conference
130 Fifth Ave.
New York, NY 10011
800-543-6786
beconference@blackenterprise.com

Professional Women in Business (PWIB)
1800 E. Garry, Suite 126
Santa Ana, CA 92705
pwib@aol.com

JUNE

The National Association of Urban Bankers
1801 K St. NW, Suite 200-1A
Washington, DC 20006
naub340@aol.com/www.naub.org

100 Black Men of America, Inc.
141 Auburn Rd.
Atlanta, GA 30303
404-688-5100
net100am@aol.com

National Insurance Association
1133 Desert Shale Ave.
Las Vegas, NV 89123
702-869-2445

National Association of Minority Contractors
666 11th St. NW
Washington, DC 20001
202-347-8259
SAMCNAMC@aol.com

National Black United Fund, Inc.
40 Clinton St.
Newark, NJ 07102
nbuf@nbuf.org

National Newspaper Publishers Association
3200 13th St. NW
Washington, DC 20010
202-588-8764
nnpadc@nnpa.org

National African American Cultural Expo
6228 N. 8th St.
Philadelphia, PA 19126
215-549-1600
Fax: 215-224-9840
NatlAACE@aol.com

National Society on Hypertension in Blacks (ISHIB)
2045 Manchester St. NE
Atlanta, GA 30324
404-875-6263
ishib@mindspring.com

National Sales Network
225 Demott Ln., Suite 2
Somerset, NJ 08873
732-246-5236
www.salesnetwork.org

JULY

Zeta Phi Beta Sorority, Inc.
1734 New Hampshire Ave. NW
Washington, DC 20009
202-387-3103
zetanatlhq@worldnet.att.net

Sigma Gamma Rho Sorority, Inc.
8800 S. Stony Island
Chicago, IL 60617
773-873-9000
ExerDSGRHO@aol.com
www.SGR1992.org

National Optometric Association
3723 Main St., Box F
E. Chicago, IL 46312
219-398-1832
CNHICKS@compuserve.com

Acapulco Black Film Festival
Uni World Films
100 Sixth Ave.
New York, NY 10013
212-219-7267
www.GOSEEBLACKMOVIES.com

National Association of Black Journalists
8701 Adelphi Rd.
Adelphi, MD 20783
301-445-7100
nabj@nabj.org

Phi Beta Sigma Fraternity, Inc.
145 Kennedy St. NW
Washington, DC 20011

202-726-5434
pbsinhq@softaid.net

Alpha Kappa Alpha Sorority, Inc.
5656 S. Stony Island
Chicago, IL 60637
773-684-1282

National Association for the Advancement
    of Colored People (NAACP)
4805 Mt. Hope Dr.
Baltimore, MD 21215
410-486-9120

Chi Eta Phi Sorority, Inc.
3029 13th St. NW
Washington, DC 20009
202-232-3858

Lambda Kappa Mu Sorority, Inc.
7302 Georgia Ave. NW, #2
Washington, DC 20012
202-829-2368
Efrandk1048@aol.com

National Association of Black Accountants, Inc.
    (NABA)
7249-A Hanover Pkwy.
Greenbelt, MD 20070
301-474-6222
www.nabainc.org

Swing Phi Swing Social Fellowship, Inc.
131-185 Bergen St., Suite 727
Newark, NJ 07103
800-707-9464
www.swingphiswing.org

American Health & Beauty Aids Institute
401 N. Michigan Ave., Suite 2400
Chicago, IL 60611
312-644-6610
ahbai@sba.com

National Association of Blacks in Criminal Justice
N.C. Central University
P.O. Box 27707
Durham, NC 27707
919-683-1801
office@nabcj.org

National Association of Negro Business &
    Professional Women's Clubs, Inc.
1806 New Hampshire Ave. NW
Washington, DC 20009
202-483-4206

National Association of Minority Automobile Dealers
    (NAMAD)
1111 14th St. NW, Suite 720
Washington, DC 20005
202-789-3140
namad-dc@msn.com

National Bar Association
1225 11th St. NW
Washington, DC 20001
202-842-3900

National Organization of Black Law Enforcement
    Executives
4609 Pinecrest Office Park Dr., Suite F
Alexandria, VA 22312
703-658-1529
noble@noblenatl.org

Alpha Phi Alpha Fraternity, Inc.
2313 St. Paul St.
Baltimore, MD 21218
410-554-0040
ALPHASJW@aol.com

National Dental Association
3517 16th St. NW
Washington, DC 20010
202-588-1697

National Urban League, Inc.
120 Wall St.
New York, NY 10005
212-558-5300

August

American Tennis Association (ATA)
8100 Cleary Blvd., Suite 1007
Plantation, FL 33324
954-382-1121
ATAFlorida@aol.com

The Association of Black Psychologists
P.O. Box 55999
Washington, DC 20040
202-722-0808
www.abpsi.org

The Association of Black Sociologists
P.O. Box 1108
Montclair, NJ 07042
212-772-5641
jbattle@shiva.hunter.cuny.edu

Iota Phi Theta Fraternity, Inc.
8602 Sweet Autumn Dr.
Baltimore, MD 21244
410-594-9744
www.IOTAPHITheta.org

National Association of Real Estate Brokers
1629 K St. NW
Washington, DC 20006
301-552-9340
www.nareb@aol.com

The Alliance of Black Lucent Employees, Inc.
P.O. Box 3063
Southfield, MI 48037
adevans@lucent.com

National Medical Association
1012 10th St. NW
Washington, DC 20001
202-347-1895

National Black Nurses Association
1511 K. St. NW, Suite 415
Washington, DC 20005
202-393-6870
NBNA@erols.com

National Primitive Baptist Convention, USA
P.O. Box 7463
Tallahassee, FL 32314
850-576-5101
natlpbconv@aol.com

National Black Police Association
3251 Mt. Pleasant St. NW
Washington, DC 20010
202-986-2070

Fax: 202-986-0410
nbpanatofc@worldnet.att.net

Blacks in Government (BIG)
1820 11th St. NW
Washington, DC 20001
202-667-3280
eason1820@aol.com

Kappa Alpha Psi Fraternity, Inc.
2322 N. Broad St.
Philadelphia, PA 19132
215-228-7184
webmaster@kapsi.org

BDPA Information Technology THOUGHT
    LEADERS
1111 14th St. NW, Suite 700
Washington, DC 20005
800-727-2372
nbdpa@IX.netcom.com

The Organization of Black Airline Pilots, Inc.
2740 Greenbriar Pkwy., Suite A-3128
Atlanta, GA 30331
800-538-6227
aviator@obap.org

Alliance of Black Telecommunications Employees, Inc.
991 U.S. Hwy 22, Suite 200
Bridgewater, NJ 08807
908-595-2100
www.abteinc.org

Mobile Merchandising Association
P.O. Box 54472
Los Angeles, CA 90054
310-967-4416

Black Enterprise/Pepsi Golf & Tennis Challenge
130 Fifth Ave.
New York, NY 10011
800-209-7229
hsutt@advantageintl.com

September

National Baptist Convention of America, Inc.
1320 Pierre Ave.
Shreveport, LA 71103
318-221-3701
nbca@shreve.net

National Association of Minorities in
    Communications
One Centerpointe Dr., Suite 410
La Palma, CA 90623
714-736-9600

Congressional Black Caucus Foundation, Inc.
1004 Pennsylvania Ave. SE
Washington, DC 20003
cbcfonline.org

The National Association of Juneteenth Lineage, Inc.
1605 E. Remington
Saginaw, MI 48601
989-752-0576
najlbg@earthlink.net

National Black MBA Association
180 N. Michigan Ave., Suite 1400
Chicago, IL 60601
chaunaci@nbmbaa.org

Consortium of Information and Telecommunications
    Executives, Inc. (CITE)
P.O. Box 58969
Philadelphia, PA 19102
215-466-4144

The International Black Women's Congress
555 Fenchurch St., Suite 102
Norfolk, VA 23510
757-625-0500
ibwconi@aol.com

OCTOBER

The Mobil African American Women on Tour
    Conference
3914 Murphy Canyon Rd., Suite 216
San Diego, CA 92123
800-560-2298
aawot@mindspring.com

National Bankers Association
1513 P St. NW
Washington, DC 20005
202-588-5432

National Association of Black Women Entrepreneurs,
    Inc. (NABWE)
P.O. Box 311299
Detroit, MI 48231
NABWE@aol.com

National Coalition of 100 Black Women, Inc.
38 W. 32nd St., Suite 1610
New York, NY 10001

212-947-2196
nc100bw@aol.com

National Black Child Development Institute
1023 15th St. NW, Suite 600
Washington, DC 20005
202-833-2220
www.nbcdl.org

National Association of Investment Companies
1111 14th St. NW, Suite 700
Washington, DC 20005
202-289-4336
jvcnaic@aol.com

National Black Media Coalition
1738 Elton Rd., Suite 314
Silver Spring, MD 20903
301-445-2600
Fax: 301-445-1693

National Council of Black Engineers and Scientists
    (NCBES)
1525 Aviation Blvd., Suite College 424
Redondo Beach, CA 90278
213-896-9779

Black Women's Network
P.O. Box 56106
Los Angeles, CA 90056

National Black Programming Consortium, Inc.
761 Oak St., Suite A
Columbus, OH 43205
nbpcinfo@blackstarcom.org

National Minority Supplier Development
    Council, Inc.
15 W. 39th St., 9th Floor
New York, NY 10018
212-944-2430
nmsdcl@aol.com

National Technical Association, Inc.
6919 N. 19th St.
Philadelphia, PA 19126
NTAMEJI@aol.com

NOVEMBER

National Pharmaceutical Association
107 Kilmayne Dr., Suite College
Cary, NC 27511
800-944-6742
tvbbamc@aol.com

American League of Financial Institutions
900 19th St. NW, Suite 400
Washington, DC 20006
202-857-3176
ALFI@acbankers.org

National Alliance of Black School Educators (NABSE)
2816 Georgia Ave. NW
Washington, DC 20001
202-608-6310
nabse@nabse.org

DECEMBER

The Whitney M. Young Jr. Memorial Conference
The Wharton School of Business
216 Vance Hall
Philadelphia, PA 19104
215-898-6180
wmy@wharton.upenn.edu

National Council of Negro Women, Inc.
633 Pennsylvania Ave. NW
Washington, DC 20004
202-737-0120

Public Relations Advertising Marketing Excellence
    Awards
10520 Riverside Dr.
Toluca Lake, CA 91602
818-761-4281